THE SONG GOES ON

COVENANT PUBLICATIONS

ISBN 910452-70-9
Copyright © June 1990 by Covenant Publications
Reprinted December 1991

COVENANT PUBLICATIONS
3200 W. Foster Avenue
Chicago, Illinois 60625
312/478-4676
800/621-1290

FOREWORD

Music is virtually universal in human cultures. It speaks of the deepest beliefs and feelings of individuals and societies. It is the chief way in which the story of a community's origin and destiny is told and retold.

The Christian Church has kept music at the heart of its life and worship from the beginning. The Psalter of the Old Testament, the knowledge of Jesus' use of hymns, and the evidence that hymns were often quoted in the New Testament itself show its centrality.

But the problem of limits is always with us. Too few of us know enough of the songs of our own tradition, let alone the richness of other traditions. Centuries of great Christian music are still largely unknown. And the explosion of new songs and hymns in our own time and cultures has produced much that is rich and valuable.

So we have produced a hymnal supplement. It is not that the old hymnals are outdated or too brief, it is simply that they are too limited. *The Song Goes On* is an evidence of our acknowledgment of our inevitable limitations. It is also a sign of our commitment to incorporate more of the great Christian music from both the past and the present into our life.

It is a tool for learning as well as praise. It is to be a companion for the piano at home as well as a companion for personal devotions. Thus it can become a treasure to the individual as well as to the Church. God grant that it be such.

Paul E. Larsen, president
The Evangelical Covenant Church

PREFACE

And from morn to set of sun
Through the Church **the song goes on.**
     Ignaz Franz 1719-1790

This phrase, taken from an eighteenth-century German text based on
the ancient hymn of the church, the "Te Deum," expresses our
intent in offering this book as a supplement to hymnals presently in
use. In a time of proliferating musical styles in hymnody—both trivial
and creative—the contents of this collection of songs represent both
continuity with the past and openness to the future while reflecting
the present.

Like the various traditions of worship itself, *The Song Goes On* is
eclectic, reflecting a broad range of hymnody such as praise choruses,
Scripture songs, gospel hymns, new translations, ethnic songs, canons,
and psalms, as well as traditional hymns. In addition to sifting the
wheat from the chaff, the committee has tried earnestly wherever
possible to be inclusive in how language is used and in the kinds of
metaphors and images employed in referring to the divine.

One will notice in the contents that the book is organized around
the basic elements of worship for the service of the Lord's Day.
However, this is a book that can also serve other settings besides Sun-
day morning worship.

The Song Goes On has been compiled by a special committee of
the Covenant Commission on Church Music and Worship. Members
of the committee are: Patricia Anderson, Richard K. Carlson, Gary
Copeland, A. Royce Eckhardt, J. Irving Erickson, Paul H. Erickson,
Kenneth L. Fenton, Marsha Foxgrover, James R. Hawkinson, Paul E.
Larsen, Jonathan D. Larson, Bryan Jeffery Leech, Roland Tabell, C.
John Weborg, and Glen V. Wiberg. Every effort has been made to
trace the ownership of all copyrights. If any omissions have occurred,
subsequent editions will be corrected on notification by copyright
holders.

Our fervent hope is that *The Song Goes On* will provide new and
fresh openings into living worship where there is a place for a broad
diversity of musical expression, thereby inspiring and enabling Chris-
tians to sing together as one choir because we are one body and
drink of one Spirit!

Glen V. Wiberg, chairperson
Commission on Church Music and Worship

James R. Hawkinson
Executive Secretary of Covenant Publications

CONTENTS

ACCOMPANIMENT

Suggested keyboard introductions are bracketed. Some songs have chord symbols (D^7/A for example). The note above the slash (D^7) is the chord to be played by upper register instruments. The note (A) below the slash is to be played by lower register instruments (bass guitar, organ pedals, left hand of keyboards, etc.). Prior thought should be given to the appropriate use of instruments, as well as the possibility of unaccompanied singing.

GATHERING

1   Christians, We Have Met to Worship

Unison

1. Chris-tians, we have met to wor-ship And a-dore the Lord our God;
2. May the Spi-rit's in-ter-ced-ing Move our hearts with ev-'ry prayer,

Will you pray with all your pow-er While we try to preach the Word?
Help us fol-low where you're lead-ing, Keep us in your ten-der care.

All is vain un-less the Spi-rit Of the Ho-ly One comes down;
Lord, we go now from this gath-'ring, Strength re-newed with hearts a-right,

Chris-tians, pray, and ho-ly man-na Will be show-ered all a-round.
To the world where you have called us; Send us forth as salt and light.

TEXT: St. 1, George Atkins; St. 2, Richard K. Carlson
MUSIC: Columbian Harmony; harm. by Norman E. Johnson
Copyright © 1989 by Covenant Publications

HOLY MANNA
8.7.8.7.D

Brothers Come, Sisters Come

2

1. Broth-ers, come;___ sis - ters, come;___ wor - ship Lord Je - sus.___
2. Trav-'ler, come;___ stran-ger, come;___ wor - ship Lord Je - sus.___
3. Broth-ers, go;___ sis - ters, go;___ wor - ship Lord Je - sus.___
4. Go and live the life he gives:___ wor - ship Lord Je - sus. As

Put a-side all that di-vides; come wor - ship the Lord.
All who fear, you're wel-come here; come wor - ship the Lord.
As we grow, our love will show we wor - ship the Lord.
we de-part, we on - ly start to wor - ship the Lord.

REFRAIN

Sing him prais - es, all God's___ peo - ple.

(1, 2) Broth-ers, come; sis - ters, come;___ wor - ship the Lord.
(3, 4) Broth-ers, go; sis - ters, go;___ wor - ship the Lord.

TEXT and MUSIC: Dan Whittemore

3 Jubilate, Everybody

Ju - bi - la - te, ev - 'ry - bod - y, Serve the
Lord in all your ways, And come be -
fore his pre - sence sing - ing. En - ter
now his courts with praise. For the Lord our
God is gra - cious, And his mer - cy's

Holy, Holy, Lord

(3-part canon)

4

I Ho - ly, ho - ly, Lord God Al - might-y; Your glo - ry fills the earth,

Lord God of hosts. *II* Ho - ly Lord God Al - might - y;

Your glo - ry fills the earth, Lord God of hosts. *III* Ho - ly

Lord God Al - might- y; Your glo - ry fills the earth, Lord God of hosts.

TEXT: Gerald S. Henderson; based on Isaiah 6:3
MUSIC: Source unknown; adapted by Gerald S. Henderson
Words © copyright 1986 WORD MUSIC (a div. of WORD, INC.).
All rights reserved. International copyright secured. Used by permission.

DONA NOBIS PACEM
Irregular meter

5

Seek Ye First

TEXT: Matthew 6:33; Deuteronomy 8:3, 7:7
MUSIC: Karen Lafferty; arr. A. Royce Eckhardt

Medley option: 5,6

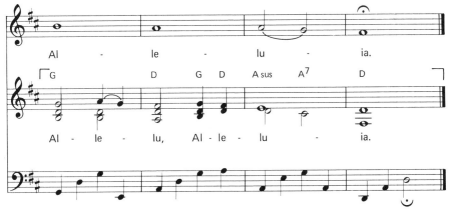

Al - le - lu - ia.

Al - le - lu, Al - le - lu - ia.

Be Still and Know

6

1. Be still and know that I am God. Be still and know that I am God. Be still and know that I am God.
2. In you, O Lord, we put our trust. In you, O Lord, we put our trust. In you, O Lord, we put our trust.

End of medley

TEXT: Psalm 46:10; 143:8
MUSIC: Composer unknown. Arr. A. Royce Eckhardt

7   Holy Is the Lord of Hosts

TEXT: Isaiah 6:3
MUSIC: Nolene Prince

Come, All Christians, Be Committed

8

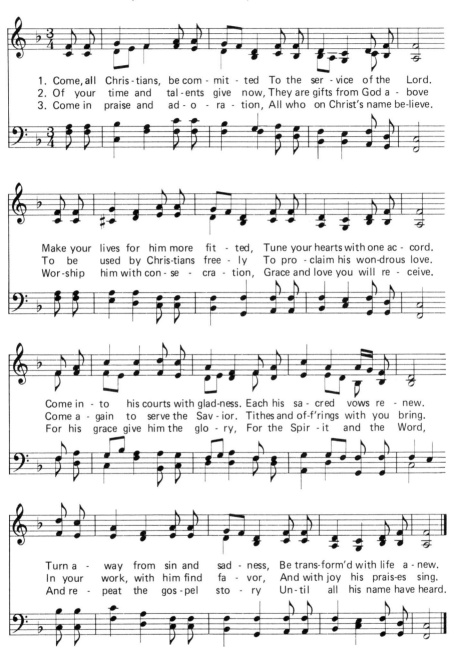

TEXT: Eva B. Lloyd, alt.
MUSIC: "The Sacred Harp," harm. by A. Royce Eckhardt

BEACH SPRING
8.7.8.7.D

9 Bless the Lord, O My Soul

TEXT: Psalm 103:1
MUSIC: Source unknown

Medley options: 9,10,11

Lift Up Your Heads

10

Medley continues: 11

*Optional E⁷ chord modulation to the key of A major.

11   He Is Lord!

He is Lord, He is Lord! He is ris-en from the dead and he is Lord! Ev-'ry knee shall bow, ev-'ry tongue con-fess, that Je - sus Christ is Lord.

End of medley

TEXT: Philippians 2:9-11
MUSIC: Traditional

12   Come, Celebrate the Presence of the Lord

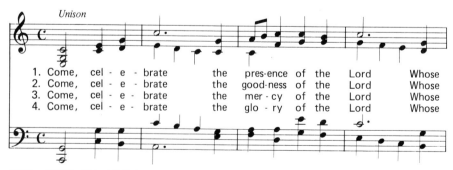

Unison

1. Come, cel - e - brate the pres-ence of the Lord Whose
2. Come, cel - e - brate the good-ness of the Lord Whose
3. Come, cel - e - brate the mer - cy of the Lord Whose
4. Come, cel - e - brate the glo - ry of the Lord Whose

TEXT and MUSIC: Richard K. Carlson
Copyright © 1989 by Richard K. Carlson. Used by permission.

OVER TEXAS
10.11.10.10.10.

13

Unto Thee, O Lord
(Psalm 25)

1. Un-to thee, O Lord,_____ do I lift up my soul._____
2. Yea, let none that wait_____ on thee be a - shamed._____

_____ do I lift up my soul._____ Un-to thee, O Lord,_
_____ on thee be a - shamed._____ Yea, let none that wait,

Un-to thee, O Lord,_____ do I lift up my
Yea, let none that wait_____ on thee be a -

_____ do I lift up my soul._____
on thee be a - shamed._____

TEXT and MUSIC: Charles Monroe, arr. Marsha Foxgrover

Let the word of Christ dwell in you richly, as you teach and admonish one another in all wisdom, and sing psalms and hymns and spiritual songs with thankfulness in your hearts to God.

Colossians 3:16, *RSV*

14   Here Before You, Lord, We Gather

1. Here be - fore you, Lord, we gath - er; God om - nip - o -
2. All things un - der your do - min - ion— Let us now hear
3. Un - to you all praise and glo - ry, Ma - jes - ty and

tent we sing. How great and ho - ly is your name, Our
your com - mand, "Be still and know that I am God, Your
hon - or due; We gath - er in your pres - ence here To

rul - er and King of kings.
times are in my hand."
love and wor - ship you.

Hear our prayer, O lov - ing Lord. Set us all a - part to

TEXT and MUSIC: Richard K. Carlson
Copyright © 1989 by Richard K. Carlson. Used by permission.

do your king-dom's work from thank-ful hearts.

Prepare the Way of the Lord
(4-part canon)

15

Pre - pare the way of the Lord. Pre - pare the way of the Lord,

and all peo-ple will see the sal - va - tion of our God. Pre -

WORDS: Isaiah 40:3; 52:10
MUSIC: Jacques Berthier and the Community of Taizé, 1984
Music © 1984 Les Presses de Taizé, by permission of G.I.A. Publications, Inc., Chicago, Illinois.

PREPARE THE WAY
Irr.

Come into His Presence
(4-part canon)

16

1. Come in - to His pres-ence sing-ing   Al - le - lu - ia,
2. Come in - to His pres-ence sing-ing   Je - sus is Lord,
3. Praise the Lord to - geth - er sing-ing   Wor - thy the Lamb,
4. Praise the Lord to - geth - er sing-ing   Glo - ry to God,

Al - le - lu - ia,   Al - le - lu - ia.
Je - sus is Lord,   Je - sus is Lord.
Wor - thy the Lamb,   Wor - thy the Lamb.
Glo - ry to God,   Glo - ry to God.

TEXT and MUSIC: Source unknown.

HIS PRESENCE
8.4.4.4.

17   The King of Glory Comes

REFRAIN

The King of glo - ry comes, the na - tion re -
joi - ces. O - pen the gates be - fore him,
lift up your voi - ces.

(last time only)   VERSES

1. Who is the King of glo - ry; what shall we call him?
2. In all of Gal - i - lee, in ci - ty or vil - lage,
3. Sing then of Da - vid's son, our Sav - ior and bro - ther;
4. He gave his life for us, the pledge of sal - va - tion.
5. He con - quered sin and death; he tru - ly has ris - en,

TEXT: Rev. W. F. Jabusch
MUSIC: Traditional Israeli folk song; arr. Betty Pulkingham
Arr. copyright © 1974, Celebration Services (Yeldall) Ltd. Text copyright by Rev. W. F. Jabusch. Used by permission.

to refrain

He is Em - man - u - el, the pro-mised of a - ges.
He goes a - mong his peo - ple cur - ing their ill - ness.
In all of Gal - i - lee was nev - er an - oth - er.
He took up - on him-self the sins of the na - tion.
And he will share with us his heav-en - ly vi - sion.

The King of glo - ry comes, the na -

tion re - joic - - - es.

Therefore, since we are surrounded by so great a cloud of witnesses, let us also lay aside every weight, and sin which clings so closely, and let us run with perseverance the race that is set before us, looking to Jesus the pioneer and perfecter of our faith, who for the joy that was set before him endured the cross, despising the shame, and is seated at the right hand of the throne of God.

Hebrews 12:1,2, *RSV*

18 Trust in the Lord

(Leader): Trust in the Lord with all your heart,

(Congregation): Trust in the Lord with

and lean not to your own un-der-stand-ing.

all your heart, and lean not to your

own un-der-stand-ing.

In all your ways ac-knowl-edge him,

In

The congregation should sing this echo song without referring to the printed music.

TEXT: Proverbs 3:5, 6
MUSIC: Roland Tabell
Copyright © 1981 by Covenant Publications.

19 In the Morning I Will Sing
(Psalm 63)

REFRAIN — *Congregation:*

In the morn-ing I will sing glad songs of praise to you.

VERSES — *Leader or choir:*

1. You are my God, I long for you from ear-ly in the morn-ing.

My whole be-ing de-sires you like a dry, worn, wa-ter-less land, My

soul thirsts for you. *(REFRAIN)* 2. In the sanc-tu-ar-y let me

TEXT: Psalm 63:1-8
MUSIC: David Goodrich

Music © 1983 by David Goodrich. Used by permission. Text adapted from Good News Bible *© 1976 by American Bible Society. Used by permission. Psalm prayer from* alive now!, *July/August 1983, © 1983 by The Upper Room.*

mem-ber you, O Lord; I think of you all night long, For

you are my con - stant help. In the sha - dow of your wings, I

sing for joy. I cling to you, your hand keeps me safe.
(REFRAIN)

PRAISE

Father, We Love You
(Glorify Thy Name)

20

TEXT and MUSIC: Donna Adkins

Medley options: 20, 21, 22, 23

21 Bless the Lord, Who Reigns in Beauty
(A Perfect Heart)

Bless the Lord,_____ who reigns in beau - ty; Bless the

Lord,_____ who reigns in wis-dom and_ with pow'r;_ Bless the

Lord, _____ who reigns my life with so much love, He can

make_____ a per - fect heart.

TEXT and MUSIC: Dony McGuire and Reba Rambo

Medley continues: 22,23

For Thou, O Lord, Art High

(We Exalt Thee)

22

TEXT: Psalm 97:9
MUSIC: Pete Sanchez, Jr.

Medley continues: 23

23   Jesus, Name Above All Names

End of medley

TEXT and MUSIC: Naida Hearn
© 1974, 78 Scripture in Song (Admin. by MARANATHA! MUSIC). All rights reserved. International copyright secured.
Used by permission.

Great Is the Lord

24

Great is the Lord, he is ho-ly and just, By his pow-er we trust in his love. _____ Great is the Lord, he is faith-ful and true, By his mer-cy he proves he is love. _____

1, 2. Great is the Lord and
D.S. Great are you, Lord, and

Medley option: 24, 25

TEXT and MUSIC: Michael W. Smith, Deborah D. Smith; arr. Marsha Foxgrover

25 How Majestic Is Your Name

TEXT and MUSIC: Michael W. Smith, arr. Marsha Foxgrover

name___ Prince of peace,___ Might-y God— O___ Lord___ God Al - might - y!___

End of medley

God Almighty, We Adore You   26
(Great Are You, O Lord)
(3-part canon)

I

1. God Al-might-y, we a - dore you, mag-ni - fy you;
2. Heav'n and earth pro-claim your pow - er, show your glo - ry;
3. Al - le - lu - ia, al - le - lu - ia, al - le - lu - ia;

II

God, our Fa - ther, we a - dore you, mag-ni - fy you;
Heav'n and earth pro-claim your pow - er, show your glo - ry;
Al - le - lu - ia, al - le - lu - ia, al - le - lu - ia;

III

Great are you, O Lord!
Great are you, O Lord!
Great are you, O Lord!

TEXT: Gerald S. Henderson
MUSIC: Traditional English melody; adapted by Gerald S. Henderson

ENGLAND
Irregular meter

27 I Will Call upon the Lord

(2-part canon)

Medley options: 27,28,29

28   I Will Sing of the Mercies of the Lord
(Psalm 89)

Medley continues: 29

TEXT: Psalm 89
MUSIC: J. H. Fillmore

With my mouth _____ will I make known thy faith-ful-ness, thy faith-ful-ness. With my mouth _____ will I make known thy faith-ful-ness to all gen-er-a-tions.

D.C. al Fine

Anyone possessed of five wits should blush with shame if he or she did not begin the day with a psalm, since even the tiniest birds open and close the day with sweet songs of holy devotion.

St. Ambrose

29   There Is Strength in the Name of the Lord
(In the Name of the Lord)

Unison

There is strength in the name of the Lord; There is pow'r in the name of the Lord;

There is hope in the name of the Lord! Bless-ed is He who comes in the

parts optional

name of the Lord. There is strength in the name of the Lord;

There is pow'r in the name of the Lord; There is hope in the

2nd time fine

name of the Lord! Bless-ed is He who comes in the name of the Lord.

End of medley

TEXT and MUSIC: Phill McHugh, Gloria Gaither and Sandi Patti Helvering; arranged by Robert F. Douglas.
Copyright © 1986 and this arr. © 1990 River Oaks Music Co./Gaither Music Co./Sandi's Songs Music. River Oaks admin.
by Meadowgreen Group, 54 Music Sq. E., Suite 305, Nashville, TN 37203. International copyright secured.
All rights reserved. Used by permission.

Behold, What Manner of Love

30

(2-part canon)

TEXT: 1 John 3:1
MUSIC: Patricia Vantine

Medley options: 30,31,32

31   Praise the Name of Jesus

Praise the name of Je - sus,

Praise the name of Je - sus, He's my rock,

He's my for - tress, He's my de-liv-er-er, in him will I trust.

Praise the name of Je - sus.

Medley continues: 32

TEXT and MUSIC: Roy Hicks

We Will Glorify

32

1. We will glo-ri-fy the King of kings, We will glo-ri-fy the Lamb; We will glo-ri-fy the Lord of lords, Who is the great I Am.
2. Lord Je-ho-vah reigns in maj-es-ty, We will bow be-fore his throne; We will wor-ship him in right-eous-ness, We will wor-ship him a-lone.
3. He is Lord of heav-en, Lord of earth, He is Lord of all who live; He is Lord a-bove the u-ni-verse, All praise to him we give.
4. Hal-le-lu-jah to the King of kings, Hal-le-lu-jah to the Lamb; Hal-le-lu-jah to the Lord of lords, Who is the great I Am.

Optional last stanza setting
Broader

give. 4. Hal-le- lu-jah to the King of kings, hal-le- lu-jah to the Lamb; Hal-le- lu-jah to the Lord of lords, who is the great I Am. Hal-le- Am.

TEXT and MUSIC: Twila Paris; arr. by David Allen

End of medley

WE WILL GLORIFY
9.7.9.6.

33   Majesty

Maj - es - ty,_____ wor-ship his maj - es - ty._____ Un - to
Je - sus be all glo - ry, hon-or, and praise._____ Maj - es - ty,_____
_____ king-dom au - thor - i - ty_____ flow from his throne un - to his own;
his an - them raise._____ So ex - alt, lift up on high the name of
Je - sus._____ Mag - ni - fy, come glo-ri - fy Christ Je-sus, the King.

TEXT and MUSIC: Jack Hayford; arr. by Eugene Thomas

MAJESTY
Irregular meter

Medley option: 33,34

Maj - es-ty, _____ wor-ship his maj - es - ty; _____
_____ Je - sus who died, now glo-ri - fied, King of all kings. _____

To God Be the Glory

34

(My Tribute)

To God be the glo - ry, To
God be the glo - ry, To

TEXT and MUSIC: Andráe Crouch; arr. Roland Tabell
Copyright 1971, Communique' Music
(Admin. by Copyright Management, Inc.)

God be the glo - ry for the things he has done!
With his blood he has saved me, with his pow'r he has raised me, To God be the glo - ry for the things he has done.

End of medley

Thou Art Worthy

35

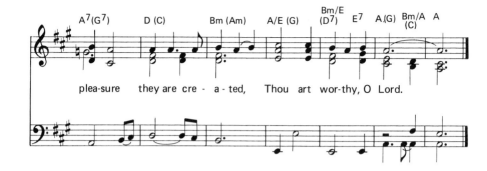

plea-sure they are cre - a - ted, Thou art wor-thy, O Lord.

36 Praise
(4-part canon)

With energy

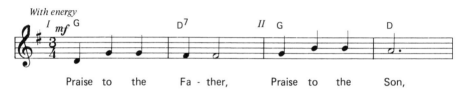

Praise to the Fa - ther, Praise to the Son,

Praise to the Spir - it, Three___ in One. Al - le -

lu - ia, al - le - lu! Al - le -

Everyone

lu - ia, al - le - lu! Al - le - lu - ia!

TEXT and MUSIC: Tom Fettke
Copyright © 1981 by Pilot Point Music.
All rights reserved. Used by permission.

When in Our Music God Is Glorified 37

Unison

1. When in our mu - sic God is glo - ri - fied,
2. How of - ten, mak - ing mu - sic, we have found
3. So has the Church, in lit - ur - gy and song,
4. And did not Je - sus sing a psalm that night
5. Let ev - 'ry in - stru-ment be tuned for praise!

And ad - o - ra - tion leaves no room for pride,
A new di - men - sion in the world of sound,
In faith and love, thro' cen - tu - ries of wrong,
When ut - most e - vil strove a - gainst the light?
Let all re - joice who have a voice to raise!

It is as though the whole cre - a - tion cried
As wor - ship moved us to a more pro - found
Borne wit - ness to the truth in ev - 'ry tongue,
Then let us sing, for whom he won the fight:
And may God give us faith to sing al - ways

1-4. Al - le - lu - ia! 5. Al - le - lu - ia!

TEXT: Fred Pratt Green
MUSIC: Charles V. Stanford

ENGELBERG
10.10.10. with Alleluia

38   Alleluia! Sing to Jesus

Unison

1. Al - le - lu - ia! sing to Je - sus;
2. Al - le - lu - ia! not as or - phans
3. Al - le - lu - ia! bread of heav - en,
4. Al - le - lu - ia! king e - ter - nal,
5. Al - le - lu - ia! sing to Je - sus;

His the scep - ter, his the throne;
Are we left in sor - row now;
Here on earth our food, our stay;
Lord om - nip - o - tent we own;
His the scep - ter, his the throne;

Al - le - lu - ia! his the tri - umph,
Al - le - lu - ia! he is near us;
Al - le - lu - ia! here the sin - ful
Al - le - lu - ia! born of Ma - ry,
Al - le - lu - ia! his the tri - umph,

His the vic - to - ry a - lone.
Faith be - lieves, nor ques - tions how.
Flee to you from day to day.
Earth your foot - stool, heav'n your throne.
His the vic - to - ry a - lone.

TEXT: William C. Dix
MUSIC: Rowland H. Prichard

HYFRYDOL
8.7.8.7.D

Hark! the songs of peace - ful Zi - on
Though the cloud from sight re - ceived him
In - ter - ces - sor, friend of sin - ners,
As with - in the veil you en - tered,
Hark! the songs of peace - ful Zi - on

Thun - der like a might - y flood:
When the for - ty days were o'er,
Earth's re - deem - er, hear our plea
Robed in flesh, our great high priest,
Thun - der like a might - y flood:

"Je - sus out of ev - 'ry na - tion
Shall our hearts for - get his pro - mise:
Where the songs of all the sin - less
Here on earth both priest and vic - tim
"Je - sus out of ev - 'ry na - tion

Has re - deemed us by his blood."
"I am with you ev - er - more"?
Sweep a - cross the crys - tal sea.
In the eu - cha - ris - tic feast.
Has re - deemed us by his blood."

39   Hosanna, Son of David!

TEXT: G. J. Vogler, based on Matthew 21:9; tr. J. Irving Erickson
MUSIC: G. J. Vogler

I Know That My Redeemer Lives

40

1. I know that my Re-deem-er lives, Think of the joy this know-ledge gives.
2. Christ gives me now his peace and love, And in - ter-cedes for me a - bove.
3. He lives, my true and trust-ed friend. Christ lives, my bro-ken-ness to mend.
4. Think of the con - se-quence of this, That ev - 'ry hon - or now is his.

O praise him, Al-le - lu - ia! Christ now has ris - en from the dead,
O praise him, Al-le - lu - ia! And when life ends, I then shall be
O praise him, Al-le - lu - ia! He lives, and while I live I'll say,
O praise him, Al-le - lu - ia! Christ lives, at this my be - ing sings,

He who once suf-fered in my stead. O praise him, O praise him,
Where he in glo - ry waits for me. O praise him, O praise him.
"Christ is my strength for each new day." O praise him, O praise him,
Christ lives to reign as King of kings; O praise him, O praise him,

Al - le - lu - ia! Al - le - lu - ia! Al - le - lu - ia! A - men.

TEXT: Bryan Jeffery Leech
MUSIC: "Geistliche Kirchensäng," Cologne; harm. Norman E. Johnson

LASST UNS ERFREUEN
LM with alleluias

41　Let All Things Now Living

1. Let all things now living A song of thanks-giv-ing
2. His law he en-forc-es, The stars in their cours-es,

To God our cre-a-tor tri-um-phant-ly raise,
The sun in its or-bit o-be-dient-ly shine;

Who fash-ioned and made us, Pro-tect-ed and stayed us,
The hills and the moun-tains, The riv-ers and foun-tains,

Who still guides us on to the end of our days.
The deeps of the o-cean pro-claim him di-vine.

TEXT: Katherine K. Davis
MUSIC: Welsh folk tune
Text copyright ©1939, E. C. Schirmer Music Co. Harm. copyright ©1978, Lutheran Book of Worship.
Reprinted by permission of Augsburg Fortress.

THE ASH GROVE
6.6.11.6.6.11.D.

His banners are o'er us, His light goes before us,
We too should be voicing Our love and rejoicing;

A pillar of fire shining forth in the night,
With glad adoration a song let us raise

Till shadows have vanished And darkness is banished,
Till all things now living Unite in thanksgiving:

As forward we travel from light into light.
"To God in the highest, hosanna and praise!"

42   Lord of All Gladness

1. Lord of all glad - ness, Ban - ish our sad - ness, Je - sus,
2. If you are ours, We fear no pow - ers, Nei - ther

sun - shine of my heart. Free-ly be - stow - ing Gifts o - ver -
dark - ness, sin, nor death. Your con-stant bless-ing, In woes dis -

flow - ing, Dwell in us and ne'er de - part. Our souls a -
tress - ing, Chang -es doubt to joy - ous faith. Tell-ing the

wak - ing, Our bond-age break - ing, Trust-ing you sure - ly
sto - ry, Sing-ing your glo - ry With heart and voic - es,

We build se - cure - ly, Rock-like for - ev - er: Al - le - lu - ia!
All heav'n re - joic - es In you for - ev - er: Al - le - lu - ia!

TEXT: Johann Lindemann, tr. Catherine Winkworth, 1858, alt. Glen V. Wiberg
MUSIC: Giovanni G. Gastoldi
Arr. copyright 1969 Concordia Publishing House. Reprinted with permission.

IN DIR IST FREUDE
PM

With ea-ger long-ing We wait your dawn-ing; Liv-ing or dy-ing,
We shout for glad-ness, Tri-umph o'er sad-ness; Songs are as-cend-ing

On you re-ly-ing, Noth-ing can sev-er: Al-le-lu-ia!
Prais-es are blend-ing In joy for-ev-er: Al-le-lu-ia!

Praise God Who Calls the Worlds to Be! 43
(Doxology)

Praise God who calls the worlds to be! Praise Je-sus Christ who makes us free!

In Ho-ly Spir-it raise the song, whose gifts u-nite and make us strong. A-men.

TEXT: Jean Lambert
MUSIC: Attr. to Louis Bourgeois
Text copyright © 1989 Jean Lambert

44 Lord, When We Praise You with Glorious Music

1. Lord, when we praise you with glo-ri-ous mu-sic;
2. Lord, when we praise you with glo-ri-ous mu-sic;
3. Lord, when we praise you with glo-ri-ous mu-sic;

Lord, when our hearts mean the things that we say;
Us-ing our gift-ed-ness sole-ly for you;
Lord, when we give you the best we can bring;

Lord, when we love you with all of our be-ing;
When we re-turn to you songs that ex-alt you;
You as Cre-a-tor en-joy our cre-a-ting;

Lord, when in faith we be-liev-ing-ly pray; Then we are
When they in-spire all the things that we do; Life has a
You as our Fa-ther take joy when we sing; Here we're be-

TEXT and MUSIC: Bryan Jeffery Leech; harm. James R. Hubbard

HUBBARD

see - ing, then we are sens - ing All that our des - ti - ny
full - ness, life has ex - cite - ment, For we are learn - ing the
gin - ning, here we're re - hears - ing Themes that in heav - en we'll

calls us to be. And in our hearts we're ex - pect - ing the
glo - ry is yours. And in our hearts we are look - ing for
ful - ly ex - plore. Prais - ing you then with a per - fect de -

mo - ment When in your pres-ence your glo - ry we'll see.
heav - en, Where we shall give you un - ceas-ing ap - plause.
vo - tion, Bow - ing be - fore you to love and a - dore.

Alleluia   45

| | G | | C | | D⁷ | | C/G G |

1. Al - le - lu - ia,   Al - le - lu - ia,   Al - le - lu - ia,   Al - le - lu - ia,
2. He's my Sav - ior,   He's my Sav - ior,   He's my Sav - ior,   He's my Sav - ior,
3. I will praise him,   I will praise him,   I will praise him,   I will praise him,

| | G | | C | | D⁷ | | C/G G |

Al - le - lu - ia, Al - le - lu - ia,   Al - le - lu - ia,   Al - le - lu - ia.
He's my Sav - ior, He's my Sav - ior,   He's my Sav - ior,   He's my Sav - ior.
I will praise him, I will praise him,   I will praise him,   I will praise him.

46   Wonderful Grace of Jesus

1. Won - der-ful grace of Je - sus, Great - er than all my sin;
2. Won - der-ful grace of Je - sus, Reach-ing to all the lost,
3. Won - der-ful grace of Je - sus, Reach-ing the most de - filed,

How shall my tongue de - scribe it, Where shall its praise be - gin?
By it I have been par - doned, Saved to the ut - ter - most;
By its trans-form-ing pow - er Mak - ing me God's dear child,

Tak - ing a - way my bur - den, Set - ting my spir - it free,
Chains have been torn a - sun - der, Giv - ing me lib - er - ty,
Pur - chas-ing peace and heav - en For all e - ter - ni - ty—

For the won - der - ful grace of Je - sus reach - es me.
For the won - der - ful grace of Je - sus reach - es me. Soft on
And the won - der - ful grace of Je - sus reach - es me. 3rd chori

CHORUS

the match-less grace of Je - sus,
Won-der-ful the match-less grace of Je - sus, Deep - er

TEXT and MUSIC: Haldor Lillenas

WONDERFUL GRACE
7.6.7.6.7.6.12. with Refrain

than the might-y roll-ing sea; Won - der-ful grace, all - suf - fi - cient for me, for e - ven me; Broad-er than the scope of my trans-gres - sions, Great-er far than all my sin and shame; O mag-ni-fy the pre-cious name of Je-sus, Praise his name!

High - er than the moun -tain, spark-ling like a foun - tain, All - suf-fi-cient grace for e - ven me; trans-gres - sions, sing it! my sin and shame;

47 Rejoice in the Lord Always

(4-part canon)

TEXT: Philippians 4:4
MUSIC: Evelyn Tarner

Medley option: 47,48

Alleluia, Alleluia, Give Thanks

48

REFRAIN

Al - le - lu - ia, al - le - lu - ia, give thanks to the ris - en Lord; Al - le -

lu - ia, al - le - lu - ia, give praise to his name.

VERSES

1. Je - sus is Lord of all the earth; He is the
2. Spread the good news o'er all the earth: Je - sus has
3. We have been cru - ci - fied with Christ; Now we shall
4. God has pro - claimed the just re - ward: Life for all
5. Come, let us praise the liv - ing God, Joy - ful - ly

king of cre - a - tion. name.
died and has ris - en.
live for - ev - er. Al - le -
peo - ple, al - le - lu - ia.
sing to our Sav - ior.

last time

End of medley

49 Praise Ye the Lord
(Psalm 150)

CONGREGATIONAL REFRAIN

Praise ye the Lord, Hal - le - lu - jah!

Lively and spirited

Ev - 'ry - bod - y praise the Lord.

Lord.

(Final time, very slow)

Omit final time

TEXT: Psalm 150:1-5
MUSIC: J. Jefferson Cleveland

Praise God   with   tim - brel   and   danc -
Praise God   with   clash - ing   cym -
Praise God   for   those   boun - ti - ful   mer -
Praise God   down   in   the   low   val -

- ing,   Praise God   wher -
- bals,   Praise God   with
- cies,   For God   ful -
- leys,   Praise God   be -

ev - er   you   are.
all   of   your   might.
fills___   our   needs.
cause   it's   all   right.

D.S. al Fine

We Are God's People

50

Unison

1. We are God's peo - ple, the cho - sen of the Lord.
2. We are God's loved ones, the bride of Christ our Lord.
3. We are the bod - y of which the Lord is head.
4. We are a tem - ple, the Spir - it's dwell - ing place.

Born of his Spir - it, es - tab-lished by his Word. Our
For we have known it, the love of God out - poured. Now
Called to o - bey him, now ris - en from the dead. He
Formed in great weak - ness, a cup to hold God's grace. We

cor - ner-stone is Christ a - lone, And strong in him we stand. O let us
let us learn how to re-turn The gift of love once giv'n. O let us
wills us be a fam - i - ly Di - verse yet tru - ly one. O let us
die a - lone, for on its own Each em - ber los - es fire; Yet joined in

live trans - par - ent-ly, And walk heart to heart and hand in hand.
share each joy and care, And live with a zeal that pleas-es heav'n.
give our gifts to God, And so shall his work on earth be done.
one the flame burns on To give warmth and light, and to in - spire.

TEXT: Bryan Jeffery Leech, based on 1 Peter 2:9.
MUSIC: Johannes Brahms; arr. Fred Bock
SYMPHONY
11.11.13.8.9.

51　Praise the Lord!

1. Praise the Lord!_ Praise, you ser-vants of the Lord,_ praise the
2. Praise the Lord!_ Thanks and prais-es sing to God,_ day by
3. Praise the Lord!_ Praise and glo-ry give to God,_ who is
4. Praise the Lord!_ Praise, you ser-vants of the Lord,_ praise the

name of the Lord!_ Bless-ed_ be the name of the Lord!_
day to the Lord!_ High a - bove the na-tions is God._
like un-to him?_ Rais-ing_ up the poor from the dust,_
love of the Lord!_ Giv-ing_ to the home-less a home,_

Bless-ed_ be the name of the Lord_ from this time forth and for -
High a - bove the na-tions is God._ his glo-ry high o - ver
Rais-ing_ up the poor from the dust,_ he makes them dwell in his
Giv-ing_ to the home-less a home,_ he fills their hearts with new

TEXT: Marjorie Jillson, based on Psalm 113
MUSIC: Heinz Werner Zimmerman

ev - er - more. Praise the Lord!__ Praise the Lord!__
earth and__ sky. Praise the Lord!__ Praise the Lord!__
heart and__ home. Praise the Lord!__ Praise the Lord!__
hope and__ joy. Praise the Lord!__ Praise the Lord!__

I See You, Lord

52

1. I see you, Lord, In all your won - drous works,
2. I know you, Lord, In man - y dif - f'rent ways:
3. I need you, Lord, So of - ten ev - 'ry day;
4. I praise you, Lord, For all your bound - less grace.

In dawn - ing day and set - ting sun; In
As Fa - ther God and sav - ing Son, As
When sin's temp - ta - tions make me fear, I
My sight and sense, my need for you, Are

friends, at home, in work be - gun; I see you, Lord.
Spir - it, who with them are one; I know you, Lord.
joy, I hope, for you are near, I need you, Lord.
swal - lowed by your love for me; I praise you, Lord!

TEXT and MUSIC: Patricia Conrad
Words and music copyright 1990 by Patricia Conrad.

DABEI
10.8.8.4.

53 Sing to the Father

(2-part canon)

1. Sing to the Fa - ther with words___ of praise, Count-ing us wor - thy to bear___ his name. Sing to the Fa-ther with words___ of love, filled with the Spir-it of life from a - bove. Hal - le - lu - jah, thank you, Lord.___ Hal - le -
2. Sing to the Sa - vior with words___ of praise, Count-ing us wor - thy to bear___ his shame. Sing to the Sav-ior with words___ of love, take up our cross and fol - low in love.
3. Sing to the Spir - it with words___ of praise, His ho - ly pres-ence with- in us pro-claim. Sing to the Spir- it with words___ of love, come fill our be - ings, O heav - en - ly Dove.

TEXT: St. 1, 2, Guy Gray; St. 3, Paul H. Erickson
MUSIC: Guy Gray

lu - jah, thank you, Lord.

Praise and Thanksgiving   54

1. Praise and thanks-giv - ing, O God we of - fer For all things
2. Bless, Lord, the la - bor We bring to serve you, That with our
3. Par - ent, pro - vid - ing Food for your chil - dren, By your wise
4. Then will your bless - ing Reach ev - 'ry peo - ple, Free - ly con -

liv - ing, Cre - at - ed good: Har - vest of sown fields, Fruits of the
neigh - bor We may be fed. Sow - ing or till - ing, We would work
guid - ing Teach us to share One with an - oth - er, So that, re -
fess - ing Your gra - cious hand. Where all o - bey you, No one will

or - chard, Hay from the mown fields, Blos - som and wood.
with you, Har - vest - ing, mill - ing For dai - ly bread.
joic - ing With us, all oth - ers May know your care.
hun - ger; In your love's sway you Nour - ish the land.

TEXT: Albert F. Bayly, alt.
MUSIC: Gaelic melody
Text copyright © Oxford University Press. Used by permission.

BUNESSAN
5.5.5.4.D

55   Sing Hallelujah to the Lord

Sing hallelujah to the Lord,
sing hallelujah to the Lord,
sing hallelujah, hallelujah,
sing hallelujah to the Lord.

1. Sing hal-le-lu-jah to the Lord,
   sing hal-le-lu-jah to the Lord,
   sing hal-le-lu-jah, sing hal-le-lu-jah,
   sing hal-le-lu-jah to the Lord.

2. Je - sus is ris-en from the dead,
   Je - sus is ris-en from the dead,
   Je - sus is ris - en, Je - sus is ris - en,
   Je - sus is ris - en from the dead.

3. Je - sus is Lord of heav'n and earth,
   Je-sus is Lord of heav'n and earth,
   Je - sus is Lord, Je - sus is Lord,
   Je - sus is Lord of heav'n and earth.

4. Je - sus is liv-ing in his Church,
   Je - sus is liv-ing in his Church,
   Je - sus is liv - ing, Je - sus is liv - ing,
   Je - sus is liv-ing in his Church.

5. Je - sus is com-ing for his own,
   Je - sus is com-ing for his own,
   Je - sus is com - ing, Je - sus is com - ing,
   Je - sus is com-ing for his own.

King of Kings and Lord of Lords

56

(2-part canon)

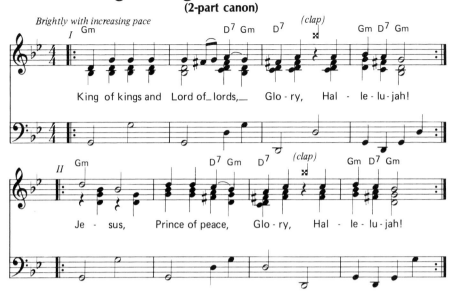

Brightly with increasing pace

I

King of kings and Lord of_lords,__ Glo - ry, Hal - le - lu - jah!

II

Je - sus, Prince of peace, Glo - ry, Hal - le - lu - jah!

TEXT: Author unknown
MUSIC: arr. Margaret Evans
Arr. Copyright © Kingsway Publications 1983.

Alleluia! Christ Is Risen

57

(3-part canon)

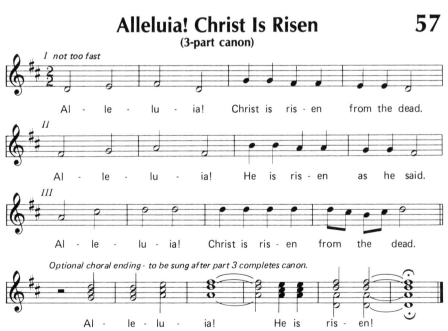

I *not too fast*

Al - le - lu - ia! Christ is ris - en from the dead.

II

Al - le - lu - ia! He is ris - en as he said.

III

Al - le - lu - ia! Christ is ris - en from the dead.

Optional choral ending - to be sung after part 3 completes canon.

Al - le - lu - ia! He is ris - en!

TEXT: Gerald S. Henderson; based on Matthew 28:6, 7
MUSIC: German Folk song; arr. by Gerald S. Henderson
Words arr. © 1986 WORD MUSIC (a div. of WORD, INC.). All Rights Reserved.
International Copyright Secured. Used by permission.

RESURRECTION CANON
11.11.11.

PRAYER

Lord, Listen to Your Children Praying 58

TEXT: Ken Medema
MUSIC: Ken Medema; arr. by Kenneth L. Fenton

Medley options: 58,59,60,61

59
Open Our Eyes

O - pen our eyes, Lord,_____ we
want to see Je - sus,_____ to reach out and
touch him,_____ and say that we
love him._____ O - pen our
ears, Lord,_____ and help us to lis -

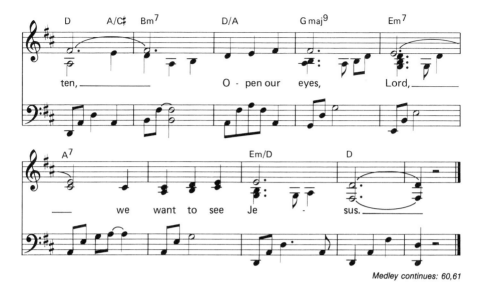

ten, _____ O - pen our eyes, Lord, _____ we want to see Je - sus. _____

Medley continues: 60,61

I Love You, Lord

60

Slowly

I love you, Lord, and I lift my voice to wor - ship you; O my soul re - joice. Take joy, my King, in

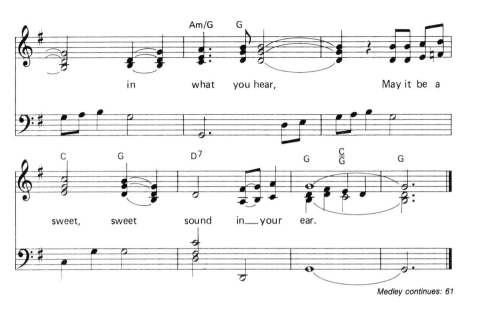

in what you hear, May it be a sweet, sweet sound in___ your ear.

Medley continues: 61

Adoramus Te

(We Adore You, O Lord)

61

O_____ A-do-ra-mus te Do-mi - ne.

Prayer of adoration
After each invocation the refrain is sung again.

Christ the Lord, you became poor and you offer the kingdom of heaven to the poor of the earth; you fill us with your riches. *Refrain*

O Lord, gentle and humble of heart, you reveal a new world to all who abandon themselves; we receive of your fullness. *Refrain*

O Lord, you fell prostrate on the ground, and you show us a path of consolation in our distress; you are the joy no one can take from us. *Refrain*

O Lord, you shed your blood, and you give the cup of life to seekers after justice; you quench every thirst. *Refrain*

O risen Lord, you showed yourself to the disciples and you pluck from our flesh our hearts of stone; we shall see you face to face. *Refrain*

O Lord, you divest the powerful and clothe peacemakers in festal robes; you transform us into your likeness. *Refrain*

O Lord, first of the living, you welcome into the kingdom of heaven all who die for you; we dwell in your love. *Refrain*

End of medley

62   Create in Me a Clean Heart

LEADER
Cre - ate in me a clean heart, O God,

CONGREGATION
And re - new a right spir - it with - in me.

LEADER
Cast me not a - way from thy pre - sence,

CONG.
And take not thy ho - ly Spir - it from me.

LEADER
Re - store to me the joy of thy sal - va - tion,

TEXT: Psalm 51:10-13
MUSIC: Jim Strathdee, arr. Marsha Foxgrover
Music © 1969 by Jim Strathdee, Desert Flower Music, P.O. Box 1735, Ridgecrest, CA 93555.
Text has been adapted from the Revised Standard Version of the Bible, copyrighted 1946, 1952, and © 1971 by the Division of Christian Education, National Council of the Churches of Christ in the United States of America, and is used by permission.

63 O Holy Spirit, Breathe on Me

Unison

1. O Ho-ly Spi - rit, breathe on me.
2. O Ho-ly Spi - rit, fill my life.
3. O Ho-ly Spi - rit, make me new.
4. O Ho-ly Spi - rit, wind of God.

O Ho-ly Spi - rit,
O Ho-ly Spi - rit,
O Ho-ly Spi - rit,
O Ho-ly Spi - rit,

breathe on me,
fill my life.
make me new.
wind of God.

And cleanse a-way my sin.
Take all my pride from me.
Make Je-sus real to me.
Give me your pow'r to-day.

Fill me with love with-in:
Give me hu-mil-i-ty:
Give me his pu-ri-ty:
To live for you al-ways.

O Ho-ly Spi - rit, breathe on me.
O Ho-ly Spi - rit, breathe on me.
O Ho-ly Spi - rit, breathe on me.
O Ho-ly Spi - rit, breathe on me.

TEXT and MUSIC: Norman Warren; arr. Kenneth Fenton.

God Is So Good

64

(A Psalm for All Seasons)

	1. God is so good.	God is so good.
Advent	2. Come, Lord Je-sus, come!	Come, Lord Je-sus, come!
Lent	3. Kind and mer-ci ful,	Kind and mer-ci - ful,
Easter	4. We praise you, O Lord!	We praise you, O Lord!
Pentecost	5. Come, O Spir-it, come!	Come, O Spir-it, come!
	6. Here am I, O Lord	Here am I, O Lord,
	7. My soul thirsts for you.	My soul thirsts for you.
	8. Praise the Lord, my soul.	Praise the Lord, my soul.
	9. Bless the Lord, my soul.	Bless the Lord, my soul.
	10. Keep us safe, O God.	Keep us safe, O God.

God is so good. He's so good to me.
Come, Lord Je-sus, come! Come and set us free!
Kind and mer-ci - ful is the Lord our God!
We praise you, O Lord for your won - drous works!
Come, O Spir - it, come; come re - new the earth.
Here am I, O Lord, I will do your will!
My soul thirsts for you, O Lord, my God.
Praise the Lord, my soul, praise his ho - ly name!
Bless the Lord, my soul, bless his ho - ly name!
Keep us safe, O God, for you are our hope!

TEXT: St. 1, Traditional; st. 2-10, Carey Landry
MUSIC: Adapted from African melody

65 God of the Prophets

1. God of the proph - ets, send us proph -ets now: Send us your Spir - it now as in the past. Each age must claim its sol - emn task and vow: Make each one no - bler, strong-er than the last!
2. A - noint them proph - ets! Make their ears at - tent To your own sa - cred speech: their hearts a - wake To hu - man need; their lips make el - o - quent To as - sure the right and ev - 'ry e - vil break.
3. A - noint them priests! Strong in - ter - ces - sors they For par - don and for char - i - ty and peace! Ah, if with them the world might pass a - stray, In - to the dear Christ's life of sac - ri - fice.
4. Make them a - pos - tles! Her - alds of your cross, Forth may they go to tell all realms your grace; In - spired of you, may they count all but loss, And stand at last with joy be - fore your face.

Adaptation of words is by Grace Moore and is used by permission.

TEXT: Denis Wortman; alt. Grace Moore
MUSIC: Abridged from *Genevan Psalter*

TOULON
10.10.10.10.

Text adapted by Grace Moore, and used by permission as published in Everflowing Streams *(The Pilgrim Press, copyright 1981, New York, NY).*

How Can We Sing the Lord's Song?
66

TEXT: Barbara Harr
MUSIC: A. Royce Eckhardt
Text copyright ©1988 Barbara Harr. Music copyright ©1989 A. Royce Eckhardt.

67

Heavenly Father
(Prayer Song)

1. Heav'n-ly Fa - ther, hal - lowed is your name. May your king - dom quick-ly come. May it be on earth just like in heav'n your per - fect will be done. Give to-day our dai - ly bread. Take a - way our sin. May your
2. Pre - cious Je - sus, how do we ex - press all the grat - i - tude we owe. For the price you paid to of - fer us sal - va - tion for our souls? When we're faced with doubt and fear, draw us close a - gain.
3. Ho - ly Spir - it, fall a - fresh on us, let our tir - ed souls re - joice. In the loud con - fus-ing life we lead, speak with your still, small voice. Be our com - fort, coun-s'lor and guide, search our hearts with - in.

TEXT and MUSIC: Richard K. Carlson
© 1985 Richard K. Carlson. Used by permission.

PRAYER SONG

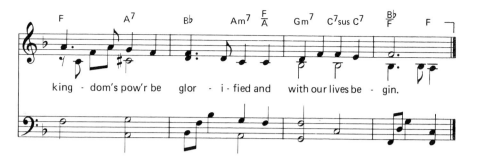

king - dom's pow'r be glor - i - fied and with our lives be - gin.

I Lift My Eyes to the Quiet Hills 68

Unison

1. I lift my eyes to the qui - et hills in the
2. I lift my eyes to the qui - et hills to a
3. I lift my eyes to the qui - et hills with a
4. I lift my eyes to the qui - et hills and my

press of a bus - y day; As green hills stand
calm that is mine to share; Se - cure and still
prayer as I turn to sleep; By day, by night,
heart to the Fa - ther's throne; In all my ways

in a dus - ty land So God is my strength and stay.
in the Fa - ther's will And kept by the Fa - ther's care.
thro' the dark and light My Shep - herd will guard his sheep.
to the end of days The Lord will pre - serve his own.

TEXT: Timothy Dudley-Smith
MUSIC: Michael Baughen

UPLIFTED EYES
9.7.9.7.

69 If My People's Hearts Are Humbled

1. If my peo-ple's hearts are hum-bled, If they pray and seek my face;
2. Then my eyes will see their sor-row, Then my ears will hear their plea.

If they turn a-way from e-vil, I will not with-hold my grace.
If my peo-ple's hearts are hum-bled, I will set their na-tion free.

I will hear their prayers from heav-en; I will par-don all who've sinned.
If my peo-ple's hearts are hum-bled, If they pray and seek my face;

If my peo-ple's hearts are hum-bled, I will sure-ly heal their land.
If they turn a-way from e-vil, I will not with-hold my grace. A-men.

TEXT: Claire Cloninger, based on 2 Chronicles 7:14
MUSIC: Rowland H. Prichard

HYFRYDOL
8.7.8.7.D.

Shine on Me

CHORUS

Shine on me, shine on me, Je - sus, shine on me.

Fine

Through the dark - ness of my heart, Je - sus, shine on me.

1. See my heart, for I re - pent; Hear my hum - ble plea
2. In your mer - cy I im-plore, Make the dark-ness flee.
3. New be - gin - nings light my way T'ward e-ter - ni - ty.

D.C. Fine

To re-new our cov - e - nant.
Heav -'nly light up - on me pour. Je - sus, shine on me.
Lead me in your light to - day.

TEXT and MUSIC: Richard K. Carlson
Copyright ©1989 Richard K. Carlson. Used by permission.

Medley option: Nos. 70, 71

71 **Bless His Holy Name**

Fine

Bless the Lord, O my soul, and all that is with-
in me bless his ho - ly name.

He has done great things, He has done great things,

D.C. al Fine

He has done great things, Bless his ho - ly name.

TEXT and MUSIC: Andraé Crouch
Copyright 1973, Communique' Music
(Admin. by Copyright Management, Inc.)

End of medley

72 **Come, Lord Jesus**

Unison

D   Gm⁷   Bm   Em

1. Come, _____ Lord Je - sus, Come, _____ Lord
2. Come, _____ O Prince of Peace, Come, _____ O
3. Our hearts are o - pen, Our hearts are
4. Come, _____ Em - man - u - el, Come, _____ Em -

TEXT AND MUSIC: Carey Landry; harm. Jonathan D. Larson
Copyright © 1976 NALR, 10802 N. 23rd Ave. Phoenix, Arizona 85029. All rights reserved. Used with permission.
Harm. copyright © 1989 Jonathan D. Larson

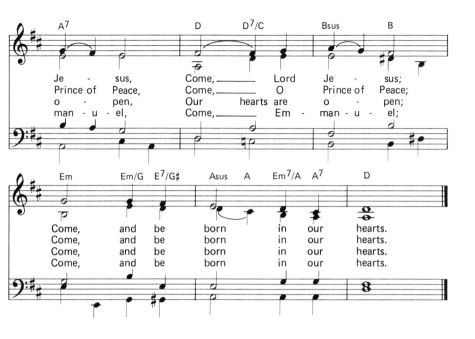

Restore in Us, O God

73

(A Lenten Prayer)

1. Re - store in us, O God, The splen - dor of your love;
2. O Spir - it, wake in us The won - der of your pow'r;
3. Bring us, O Christ, to share The full - ness of your joy;
4. Three per - soned God, ful - fill The prom - ise of your grace,

Re - new your im - age in our hearts, And all our sins re - move.
From fruit-less fear un - furl our lives Like spring-time bud and flow'r.
Bap - tize us in the ris - en life That death can-not de - stroy.
That we, when all our search-ing ends, May see you face to face. A-men.

TEXT: Carl P. Daw, Jr.
MUSIC: Johann Martin Spiess
SWABIA
S.M.

74   Lead On, O Cloud of Presence

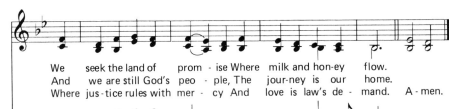

1. Lead on, O cloud of Pres - ence, The ex - o - dus is come;
2. Lead on, O fi - ery pil - lar, We fol - low yet with fears,
3. Lead on, O God of free - dom, And guide us on our way;

In wil - der - ness and des - ert Our tribe shall make its home.
But we shall come re - joic - ing Though joy be born of tears.
Though those who start the jour - ney Know strug - gle and de - lay,

Our bond - age left be - hind us, New hopes with-in us grow,
We are not lost though wan-der-ing, For by your light we come,
We pray our sons and daugh - ters May live to see that land

We seek the land of prom - ise Where milk and hon-ey flow.
And we are still God's peo - ple, The jour-ney is our home.
Where jus-tice rules with mer - cy And love is law's de - mand. A - men.

TEXT: Ruth Duck
MUSIC: Melchior Teschner
Text copyright © 1974 by Ruth Duck. Used by permission.

ST. THEODULPH
7.6.7.6.D.

My God, When I Consider

75

1. My God, when I con-si-der What you have done for me, The
2. Thro' ag-o-ny and suf-f'ring You bore my ev-'ry sin, And
3. How blest to have this treas-ure As fore-taste of my home, The
4. Why should I then be griev-ing When hav-ing such a friend? No,

grace you dai-ly of-fer That I in won-der see. My
o-ver me kept watch-ing, My wan-d'ring heart to win. Would
joy that knows no mea-sure Is mine in you a-lone. Your
rath-er I'd be sing-ing Un-til my jour-ney's end. So

heart is filled with rap-ture, With joy your name I laud, All
life be worth the liv-ing, What fu-ture could I know, If
lov-ing hand pro-tects me, Your grace— each morn-ing new; 'Mid
I will sound your prais-es Of faith-ful-ness and grace; I'll

praise my heav'n-ly Fa-ther, All praise dear Lamb of God.
I were not for-giv-en, And grace were not be-stowed?
per-ils of the jour-ney I find your prom-ise true.
sing through end-less ag-es Be-yond all time and space.

TEXT: Nils Frykman; tr. Signe L. Bennett and Glen V. Wiberg
MUSIC: From "Hemlandsånger," 1877
Text copyright © 1981 by Covenant Publications

MARVEL
7.6.7.6.D.

76   O Christ, the Healer, We Have Come

1. O Christ, the heal - er, we have come To pray for health, to plead for friends. How can we fail to be re-stored When reached by love that nev - er ends?

2. From ev - 'ry ail - ment flesh en - dures Our bod - ies clam - or to be freed; Yet in our hearts we would con - fess That whole-ness is our deep-est need.

3. In con - flicts that de - stroy our health We rec - og - nize the world's dis-ease; Our com - mon life de - clares our ills. Is there no cure, O Christ, for these?

4. Grant that we all, made one in faith, In your com - mu - ni - ty may find The whole-ness that, en - rich - ing us, Shall reach and pros - per hu - man - kind. A - men.

TEXT: Fred Pratt Green
MUSIC: W. Walker, Southern Harmony, harm. Marsha Foxgrover
Text copyright 1969 by Hope Publishing Company, Carol Stream, IL 60188. All rights reserved. Used by permission.
Harm. copyright 1990 by Marsha Foxgrover.

DISTRESS
LM

Lord, Who Throughout These Forty Days   77

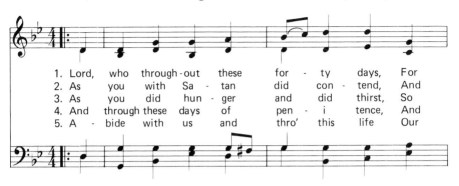

1. Lord, who through-out these for - ty days, For
2. As you with Sa - tan did con - tend, And
3. As you did hun - ger and did thirst, So
4. And through these days of pen - i - tence, And
5. A - bide with us and thro' this life Our

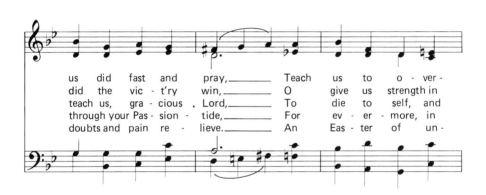

us did fast and pray,_____ Teach us to o - ver -
did the vic - t'ry win,_____ O give us strength in
teach us, gra - cious . Lord,_____ To die to self, and
through your Pas - sion - tide,_____ For ev - er - more, in
doubts and pain re - lieve._____ An Eas - ter of un -

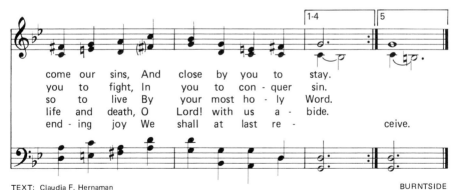

come our sins, And close by you to stay.
you to fight, In you to con - quer sin.
so to live By your most ho - ly Word.
life and death, O Lord! with us a - bide.
end - ing joy We shall at last re - ceive.

TEXT: Claudia F. Hernaman
MUSIC: Jonathan D. Larson
Music copyright ©1989 Jonathan D. Larson

BURNTSIDE
8.6.8.6.

78 Precious Lord, Take My Hand

1. Pre-cious Lord, take my hand, Lead me on, let me stand, I am tired, I am weak, I am worn; Thro' the storm, thro' the night, Lead me on to the light, Take my
2. way grows drear, Pre-cious Lord, lin-ger near, When my life is al-most gone, Hear my cry, hear my call, Hold my hand lest I fall, Take my
3. dark-ness ap-pears, And the night draws near, And my day is past and gone, At the ri-ver I stand, Guide my feet, hold my hand; Take my

TEXT: Thomas A. Dorsey
MUSIC: George N. Allen; arr. Marsha Foxgrover

PRECIOUS LORD
Irregular

hand, pre-cious Lord, lead me home.
hand, pre-cious Lord, lead me home. 2. When my
hand, pre-cious Lord, lead me home. 3. When the

I Want Jesus to Walk with Me 79

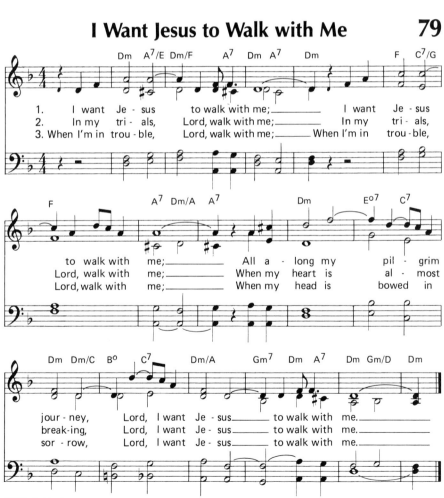

1. I want Je - sus to walk with me;____ I want Je - sus
2. In my tri - als, Lord, walk with me;____ In my tri - als,
3. When I'm in trou - ble, Lord, walk with me;____ When I'm in trou - ble,

to walk with me;____ All a - long my pil - grim
Lord, walk with me;____ When my heart is al - most
Lord, walk with me;____ When my head is bowed in

jour - ney, Lord, I want Je - sus____ to walk with me.
break - ing, Lord, I want Je - sus____ to walk with me.
sor - row, Lord, I want Je - sus____ to walk with me.

TEXT: Spiritual
MUSIC: Traditional; harm. J. Jefferson Cleveland and Verolga Nix.
Harm. copyright © 1981 by Abingdon Press. Used by permission from Songs of Zion.

80   Shine on My Life with Your Love

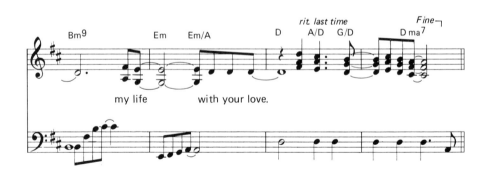

TEXT and MUSIC: Bob Stromberg, arr. Richard K. Carlson

1. God's true vine, limbs in - ter - twined, root-ed in
2. When I fall, Je - sus, be all that you have
3. When I'm strong, Lord, may I long to see you more
4. In the end call me your friend and faith-ful

glo - ry. May I see your life in
prom - ised. Cleanse my heart, Lord, let me
clear - ly. Know - ing you are who you
foll'w - er. Shin - ing bright a rad - iant

me blos - som - ing with love.
start a - new to - day.
say you are to - day.
light ev - er in your love.

D.C. al Fine

Father, I Adore You

81

(3-part canon)

1. Fa - ther, I a - dore you, Lay my life be - fore you— How I love you!
2. Je - sus, I a - dore you, Lay my life be - fore you— How I love you!
3. Spir-it, I a - dore you, Lay my life be - fore you— How I love you!

TEXT and MUSIC: Terrye Coelho

82   There Is a Road That Goes to Heaven

1. There is a road that goes to heav'n, A
2. There is a road to Je - sus' prayer, Like
3. And if you want to walk that way, On
4. There is a road that goes to heav'n, A

road to God's Je - ru - sa - lem. That road is faith's re -
him it has a ra - diance fair. What none has seen or
his own word you can re - ly; But do not doubt, be
road to God's Je - ru - sa - lem. Right here, right now, it

li - ance strong On Je - sus Christ, God's on - ly Son.
ev - er heard He has brought down to low - ly earth.
bold in trust! There is a bridge from faith to rest.
may be trod; Where - 'er it goes, it goes to God.

TEXT: Bo Setterlind, 1972; tr. Karl Olsson
MUSIC: Swedish folk melody; harm. Gunno Södersten

PROCLAMATION

There Is a Redeemer

83

1. There is a re - deem - er, Je - sus, God's own Son;
2. Je - sus, my re - deem - er, Name a - bove all names;
3. When I stand in glo - ry, I will see his face,

Pre - cious Lamb of God, Mes-si - ah, Ho - ly One.
Pre - cious Lamb of God, Mes-si - ah, O for sin - ners slain.
There I'll serve my king for - ev - er In that ho - ly place.

REFRAIN

Thank you, O my Fa - ther, For giv-ing us your Son, And

leav - ing your Spir - it Till the work on earth is done.

TEXT and MUSIC: Melody Green; arr. Keith Phillips

GREEN
Irregular meter

84 Lift High the Cross

REFRAIN *Unison*

Lift high the cross, the love of Christ pro - claim Till
all the world a - dore his sa - cred name.

Parts

1. Come, Chris - tians, fol - low where our Sav - ior trod,
2. Led on their way by this tri - um - phant sign,
3. O Lord, once lift - ed on the glo - rious tree,
4. So shall our song of tri - umph ev - er be:

Our king vic - to - rious, Christ, the Son of God.
The hosts of God in con - qu'ring ranks com-bine.
As thou hast prom - ised, draw us all to thee.
Praise to the Cru - ci - fied for vic - to - ry.

Fine

D.C. al Fine

TEXT: George W. Kitchin, alt. Michael R. Newbolt
MUSIC: Sydney H. Nicholson

CRUCIFER
10.10.10.10.

Christ Is Alive! 85

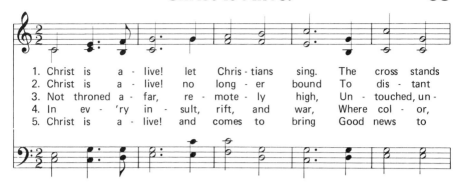

1. Christ is a - live! let Chris - tians sing. The cross stands
2. Christ is a - live! no long - er bound To dis - tant
3. Not throned a - far, re - mote - ly high, Un - touched, un -
4. In ev - 'ry in - sult, rift, and war, Where col - or,
5. Christ is a - live! and comes to bring Good news to

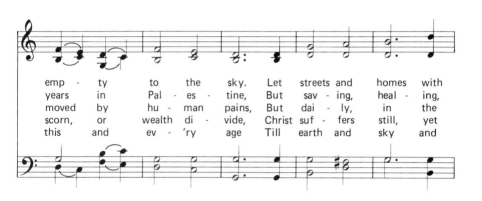

emp - ty to the sky. Let streets and homes with
years in Pal - es - tine, But sav - ing, heal - ing,
moved by hu - man pains, But dai - ly, in the
scorn, or wealth di - vide, Christ suf - fers still, yet
this and ev - 'ry age Till earth and sky and

prais - es ring. Love drowned in death shall nev - er die.
here and now, And touch - ing ev - 'ry place and time.
midst of life, Our Sav - ior in the God - head reigns.
loves the more, And lives, where e - ven hope has died.
o - cean ring With joy, with jus - tice, love, and praise.

TEXT: Brian Wren
MUSIC: Thomas Williams, *Psalmodia Evangelica*, 1789

TRURO
LM

86   **In Early Morn**

1. In   ear - ly morn the glis - t'ning dew Greets all   the
2. The   ri - sing sun shines thro' the day To warm and
3. Thus we who see the ho - ly pow'r A   whis - pered
4. From dawn of hope to dusk of day God, like a
5. Praise God from whom all bles - sings flow, Praise him all

world with life a - new; Thus Spi - rit si - lent
bright - en jour - ney's way; So ev - er ra - diant
grace on ev - 'ry flow'r Must here on earth let
fa - ther, guards the way; Then, like a mo - ther,
crea - tures here be - low; Praise him a - bove you

from a - bove A - noints the world with hope and love.
heav'n - ly grace Warms heart to heart, shines face to face.
oth - ers see The pres - ence of e - ter - ni - ty.
child at breast, God lays her chil - dren down to rest.
heav'n - ly host, Praise Fa - ther, Son, and Ho - ly Ghost.

TEXT: Dennis P. Moon, sts. 1-4; Thomas Ken, st. 5
MUSIC: Dennis P. Moon
Copyright © 1990 by Dennis P. Moon

At the Name of Jesus

Unison

1. At the name of Je - sus
2. Hum-bled for a sea - son
3. Cel - e - brate his tri - umph
4. In your hearts en - throne him,
5. Chris-tians, this Lord Je - sus

1. Ev - 'ry knee shall bow,
2. To re - ceive a name
3. With love as strong as death
4. There let him sub - due
5. Shall re - turn a - gain

Ev - 'ry tongue con - fess him King of glo - ry___ now:
From the lips of sin - ners Un-to whom he___ came,
And with awe and won - der And with bat - ed___ breath:
All that is not ho - ly, All that is not___ true;
With the Fa - ther's glo - ry, When he comes to___ reign.

'Tis the Fa - ther's plea-sure We should call him Lord,
Faith-ful - ly he bore it Spot-less to the last,
He is God our Sav - ior, He is Christ the Lord,
Crown him as your sov' - reign In temp - ta - tion's hour,
For all earth - ly pow - ers Soon to him must bow

Who from the be - gin - ning Was the might - y Word.
Brought it back vic - to - rious When from death he passed.
Al - ways to be wor-shiped, Trust-ed and a - dored.
Let his will en - fold you In its might - y pow'r.
So let us con - fess him King of glo - ry now.

TEXT: Caroline Maria Noel, alt. Based on Philippians 2:5-11
MUSIC: John Michael Brierley

CAMBERWELL
6.5.6.5.D

88   How Lovely Is Your Dwelling Place

How love - ly is your dwell - ing place, O

Lord God of hosts!_____ 1. My soul yearns and 2. How hap - py are 3. O Lord_____ of

pines for the courts of the Lord, my heart and my
they who may dwell in your courts, how hap - py when
hosts, _____ hear_____ my cry, and heark - en, O

TEXT: Psalm 84
MUSIC: Michael Joncas

flesh___ cry out;_____ E - ven the spar - row may
you are their strength;_____ Though they might go through the
God___ of love;_____ One day in your house is worth

find___ a home, the swal - low a nest for her young;___
val - ley of death, they make it a place___ of springs.___
much more to me than ten thou - sand an - y - where else.___

_____ Your al - tars, my king and my God!
_____ Your first rain will bring it to life.
_____ The Lord is my sun and my shield!

rit.   *D.C. al Fine*

rit.

89   Creating God, Your Fingers Trace

1. Cre - a - ting God, your fin - gers trace the bold de -
2. Sus - tain - ing God, your hands up - hold earth's mys-t'ries
3. Re - deem - ing God, your arms em - brace all now de -
4. In - dwell - ing God, your Gos - pel claims one fam - 'ly

signs of far - thest space; Let sun and moon and stars and
known or yet un - told; Let wa - ter's fra - gile blend with
spised for creed or race; Let peace de - scend - ing like a
with a bil - lion names; Let ev - 'ry life be touched by

light and what lies hid - den praise your might.
air, en - a - bling life, pro - claim your care.
dove, make known on earth your heal - ing love.
grace un - til we praise you face to face. A - men.

TEXT: Jeffery Rowthorn
MUSIC: William Gardiner's "Sacred Melodies," 1815.
Text copyright © 1979 by The Hymn Society, Texas Christian University, Fort Worth, TX 76129.
All rights reserved. Used by permission.

GERMANY
L.M.

90   Sing of Eve and Sing of Adam

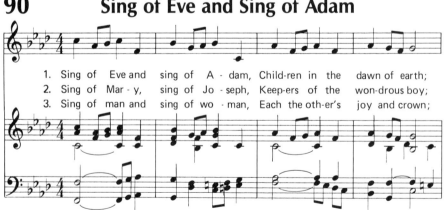

1. Sing of Eve and sing of A - dam, Child-ren in the dawn of earth;
2. Sing of Mar - y, sing of Jo - seph, Keep-ers of the won-drous boy;
3. Sing of man and sing of wo - man, Each the oth-er's joy and crown;

TEXT: T. Herbert O'Driscoll. Used by permission.
MUSIC: George Henry Day. Used by permission of Church Pension Fund.

GENEVA
8.7.8.7.D.

Who with dust and death with-in them, Yet by God were giv - en birth.
Called by God to high vo - ca - tion, Shar-ing sor - row, shar-ing joy.
Male and fe - male, both trans-fig-ured In the Lord of life come down.

Side by side they named cre - a - tion, Both from E - den's peace were hurled,
Shar-ing love, and by that lov - ing In their home in Naz - a - reth,
Called to e - qual co - re - la - tion, Where their gifts be - com - ing one

Liv - ing in their pain and pas-sion All the sto- ry of the world.
Form-ing one whose grace and glo - ry Suf-fered, died, and con-quered death.
Bring to birth a new cre - a - tion, And the will of God is done.

91

Long-time ago in Bethlehem
(Mary's Little Boy Child)

1. Long-time a-go in Beth - le-hem,____ so the Ho - ly
2. Shep-herds watched their flocks by night,_they saw a bright new
3. Jo - seph and his wife, Ma-ry, ____ came to Beth - le -
4. By and by they found a lit - tle nook____ in a sta - ble

Bi - ble say,____ Mar - y's boy child,
shin - ing star,____ And heard a choir from
hem that night.____ They found no place to
all for-lorn,____ And in a man - ger,

Je - sus Christ____ was born on Christ - mas Day.
heav - en sing,____ the mus - ic came from a - far.
bear her child,____ not a sin - gle room was in sight.
cold and dark,____ Mar - y's lit - tle boy child was born.

TEXT and MUSIC: Jester Hairston

92   On This Day Earth Shall Ring

1. On this day   earth shall ring
2. His the doom,   ours the mirth;
3. God's bright star,   o'er his head,
4. On this day   an - gels sing;

With the song   chil - dren sing   To the Lord,   Christ our King,
When he came   down to earth   Beth-le - hem   saw his birth;
Wise men three   to him led;   Kneel they low   by his bed,
With their song   earth shall ring,   Prais-ing Christ,   heav - en's King,

Born on earth to   save   us;   Him the Fa - ther   gave   us.
Ox and ass be - side   him   From the cold would   hide   him.
Lay their gifts be - fore   him,   Praise him and a - dore   him.
Born on earth to   save   us;   Peace and love he   gave   us.

TEXT: Piae Cantiones; tr. by Jane M. Joseph
MUSIC: Composer unknown; arr. by Gustav T. Holst

PERSONENT HODIE
6.6.6.6.6. with refrain

REFRAIN

*Id - e - o - o - o, Id - e - o - o - o.

Id - e - o Glo - ri - a in ex - cel - sis De - o!

* Ideo (ee-deh-oh) = therefore

Gloria, Gloria
(4-part canon)

93

I F Gm⁷ C⁷ F II Gm⁷ C⁷ F

Glo - ri - a, glo - ri - a, in ex - cel - sis De - o!

III F Gm⁷ C⁷ F IV Gm⁷ C⁷ F

Glo - ri - a, glo - ri - a! Al - le - lu - ia! Al - le - lu - ia!

TEXT: Luke 2:14
MUSIC: Jacques Berthier and the Community of Taizé, 1979
Music © 1979 Les Presses de Taizé by permission of G.I.A. Publications, Inc., Chicago, IL

GLORIA CANON
Irr.

94 Sing We Now of Christmas

Unison

1. Sing we now of Christ - mas, Sing we here No - el! Of our Lord and Sa - vior We the tid - ings tell. Sing we No - el! For Christ is born, No - el!
2. An - gels then did say, "O shep-herds come and see, Born in Beth-le - hem, A bless-ed lamb for thee." Sing we No - el! For Christ is born, No - el!
3. In the man - ger bed, The shep-herds found the child. Jo - seph too was there, And Ma - ry mo - ther mild. Sing we No - el! For Christ is born, No - el!
4. Ma - gi or - i - en - tal jour-neyed from a - far. They did come to greet him 'Neath the shin - ing star. Sing we No - el! For Christ is born, No - el!

Sing we now of Christ-mas, Sing we here No-el!

TEXT: Noel Nouvelet, tr. Richard Zgodava
MUSIC: French carol
NOEL NOUVELET
11.10.10.11.

Text sts. 1,4 copyright © 1966 Augsburg Publishing House. Reprinted by permission of Augsburg Fortress.
Music from the Oxford Book of Carols, by permission of Oxford University Press.

95 Now the Green Blade Rises

1. Now the green blade rises from the buried grain,
   Wheat that in dark earth many days has lain;
   Love lives again that with the dead has been;
   Love is come again like wheat arising green.

2. In the grave they laid him, love by hatred slain,
   Thinking that he would never wake again,
   Laid in the earth like grain that sleeps unseen;
   Love is come again like wheat arising green.

3. Forth he came at Easter, like the risen grain,
   He that for three days in the grave had lain;
   Raised from the dead, my living Lord is seen;
   Love is come again like wheat arising green.

4. When our hearts are win-try, grieving, or in pain,
   Your touch can call us back to life again,
   Fields of our hearts that dead and bare have been;
   Love is come again like wheat arising green.

TEXT: J. M. C. Crum, to be sung to the NOEL NOUVELET tune above.

He's Alive! 96
(3-part canon)

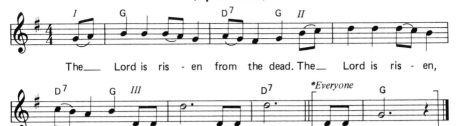

The__ Lord is ris - en from the dead. The__ Lord is ris - en,
as__ he said. He's a - live! He's a - live! He's a - live!

*After voice III has completed the third phrase the last time.

TEXT and MUSIC: Tom Fettke

When Christ Was Lifted from the Earth 97

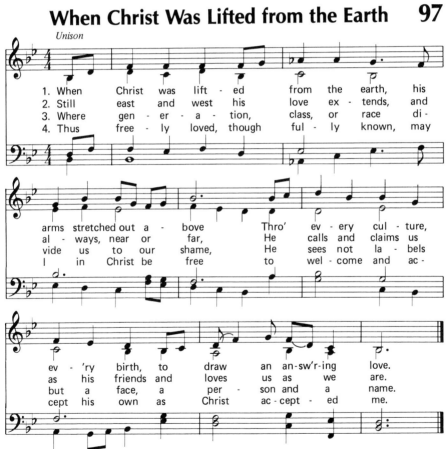

Unison

1. When Christ was lift - ed from the earth, his
2. Still east and west his love ex - tends, and
3. Where gen - er - a - tion, class, or race di -
4. Thus free - ly loved, though ful - ly known, may

arms stretched out a - bove Thro' ev - ery cul - ture,
al - ways, near or far, He calls and claims us
vide us to our shame, He sees not la - bels
I in Christ be free to wel - come and ac -

ev - 'ry birth, to draw an an - sw'r - ing love.
as his friends and loves us as we are.
but a face, a per - son and a name.
cept his own as Christ ac - cept - ed me.

TEXT: Brian Wren
MUSIC: Spiritual, arr. by Harry T. Burleigh

BURLEIGH
C.M.

98   You That Know the Lord Is Gracious

1. You that know the Lord is gra - cious,
2. Liv - ing stones by God ap - point - ed
3. Tell the praise of him who called you

You for whom a cor - ner - stone
Each to their al - lot - ted place,
Out of dark - ness in - to light,

Stands of God e - lect and pre - cious,
Kings and priests, by God a - noint - ed,
Broke the fet - ters that en - thralled you,

Laid that you may build there - on,
Shall you not de - clare his grace?
Gave you free - dom, peace, and sight:

TEXT: C. A. Alington
MUSIC: Cyril V. Taylor

ABBOT'S LEIGH
8.7.8.7.D.

Text copyright by Hope Publishing Company.

See that on that sure____ foun - da - tion
You, a roy - al gen - er - a - tion,
Tell the tale of sins____ for - giv - en,

You a liv - ing tem - ple raise—
Tell the tid - ings of your birth,
Strength re - newed____ and hope re - stored,

Tow - ers that may tell forth____ sal - va - tion,
Tid - ings of a new____ cre - a - tion
With____ the earth, in tune____ with heav - en,

Walls____ that may____ re - ech - o praise.
To____ an old____ and wea - ry earth.
Praise____ and mag - ni - fy the Lord.

99   Marvelous Grace of Our Loving Lord

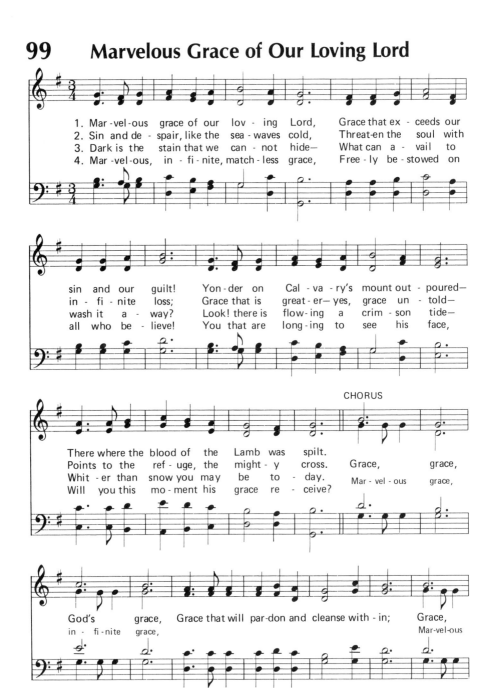

1. Mar-vel-ous grace of our lov-ing Lord, Grace that ex-ceeds our
2. Sin and de-spair, like the sea-waves cold, Threat-en the soul with
3. Dark is the stain that we can-not hide— What can a-vail to
4. Mar-vel-ous, in-fi-nite, match-less grace, Free-ly be-stowed on

sin and our guilt! Yon-der on Cal-va-ry's mount out-poured—
in-fi-nite loss; Grace that is great-er—yes, grace un-told—
wash it a-way? Look! there is flow-ing a crim-son tide—
all who be-lieve! You that are long-ing to see his face,

CHORUS

There where the blood of the Lamb was spilt.
Points to the ref-uge, the might-y cross. Grace, grace,
Whit-er than snow you may be to-day. Mar-vel-ous grace,
Will you this mo-ment his grace re-ceive?

God's grace, Grace that will par-don and cleanse with-in; Grace,
in-fi-nite grace, Mar-vel-ous

TEXT: Julia H. Johnston
MUSIC: Daniel B. Towner

MOODY
9.9.9.9. with refrain

grace, God's grace, Grace that is great-er than all our sin!
grace, in - fi - nite grace,

Let God Be God 100

Unison

1. Let God be God in this our pres-ent mo-ment. Let God be mas-ter hold-ing
2. Let God be God, or we shall nev - er fin - ish The task to which he calls us
3. Let Christ be Lord in all his ris - en pow - er; His gra-cious Spir-it un - sup -
4. Let this be ours as we a - wait his com-ing, To tell the world of him our

in con-trol All parts of life as gifts of his be - stow-ment
ev - 'ry day; Lest, err - ing, we in un - be - lief di - min - ish
pressed and free; Our Fa-ther, re - cre-ate us for this hour
Lord and King; O let us march to this, the dis - tant drum - ming

CODA (after stanza 4)

For mak-ing those now bro-ken strong and whole.
The force, the pow'r God wish-es to dis-play.
In - to the church you wish for us to be.
Which in cre-scen-do soon will roar and ring. Let God be God, let Christ be King!

TEXT and MUSIC: Bryan Jeffery Leech

CARLA
11.10.11.10.

101   Lord of All Hopefulness

1. Lord of all hope-ful-ness, Lord of all joy, Whose
2. Lord of all ea - ger - ness, Lord of all faith, Whose
3. Lord of all kind - li - ness, Lord of all grace, Your
4. Lord of all gen - tle - ness, Lord of all calm, Whose

trust, ev - er child - like, no cares could des - troy. Be
strong hands were skilled at the plane and the lathe, Be
hands swift to wel - come, your arms to em - brace, Be
voice is con - tent - ment, whose pres - ence is balm, Be

there at our wak - ing, and give us, we pray, Your
there at our la - bors, and give us, we pray, Your
there at our hom - ing, and give us, we pray, Your
there at our sleep - ing, and give us, we pray, Your

bliss in our hearts, Lord, at the break of the day.
strength in our hearts, Lord, at the noon of the day.
love in our hearts, Lord, at the eve of the day.
peace in our hearts, Lord, at the end of the day.

TEXT: Jan Struther
MUSIC: Traditional Irish melody
From "Enlarged Songs of Praise" by permission of Oxford University Press.

SLANE
10.11.11.12.

Sometimes a Light Surprises

1. Some-times a light sur - pris - es The child of God who sings;
2. In ho - ly con-tem - pla - tion We sweet-ly then pur - sue
3. It can bring with it noth - ing, But God will bear us through;
4. Though vine nor fig tree nei - ther Their wont-ed fruit should bear,

It is the Lord, who ris - es With heal-ing in his wings.
The theme of God's sal - va - tion, And find it ev - er new;
Who gives the lil - ies cloth - ing Will clothe his peo - ple too.
Though all the fields should with - er, Nor flocks nor herds be there;

When com-forts are de - clin - ing, God grants the soul a - gain
Set free from pres - ent sor - row, We cheer-ful - ly can say,
Be - neath the spread-ing heav - ens No crea - ture but is fed;
Yet, God the same a - bid - ing, His praise shall tune my voice;

A sea - son of clear shin - ing, To cheer it af - ter rain.
"Let the un - known to - mor - row Bring with it what it may."
And he who feeds the ra - vens Will give his chil - dren bread.
For, while in him con - fid - ing, I can - not but re - joice.

TEXT: William Cowper, alt.
MUSIC: Swedish "Koralbok," 1697

BLOMSTERTID
7.6.7.6.D.

103 Though I May Speak with Bravest Fire
(The Gift of Love)

1. speak _____ with brav - est fire, And have the
2. give _____ all I pos - sess, And striv-ing
3. come, _____ our hearts con - trol, Our spir-its

3. Come, Spir-it, come, _____ our hearts con - trol,

gift _____ to all in - spire,
so _____ my love pro - fess,
long _____ to be made whole.

our spir - its long _____ to be made _____

TEXT and MUSIC: Hal Hopson, based on 1 Corinthians 13 and an American Folk Tune
Copyright © 1972 by Hope Publishing Company, Carol Stream, IL 60188.
All rights reserved. Used by permission.

GIFT OF LOVE
L.M.

104 Christ Loves the Church

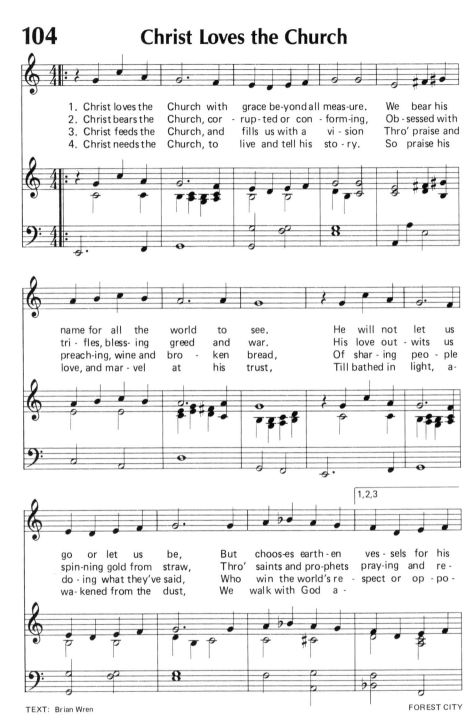

1. Christ loves the Church with grace be-yond all meas-ure. We bear his
2. Christ bears the Church, cor - rup-ted or con - form-ing, Ob - sessed with
3. Christ feeds the Church, and fills us with a vi - sion Thro' praise and
4. Christ needs the Church, to live and tell his sto - ry. So praise his

name for all the world to see. He will not let us
tri - fles, bless- ing greed and war. His love out - wits us
preach-ing, wine and bro - ken bread, Of shar - ing peo - ple
love, and mar - vel at his trust, Till bathed in light, a-

go or let us be, But choos-es earth - en ves - sels for his
spin-ning gold from straw, Thro' saints and pro-phets pray-ing and re-
do - ing what they've said, Who win the world's re - spect or op - po-
wa - kened from the dust, We walk with God a-

FOREST CITY

TEXT: Brian Wren
MUSIC: Marsha Foxgrover
Text copyright 1986 by Hope Publishing Company, Carol Stream, IL 60188. All rights reserved. Used by permission.
Music copyright 1990 by Marsha Foxgrover.

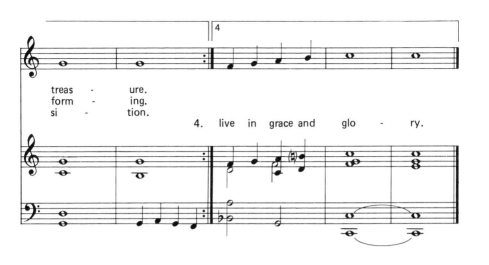

treas - ure.
form - ing.
si - tion.

4. live in grace and glo - ry.

The Care the Eagle Gives Her Young   105

1. The care the ea - gle gives her young, Safe in her lof - ty nest,
2. As when the time to ven-ture comes, She stirs them out to flight,
3. And if we flut - ter help-less-ly, As fledg-ling ea - gles fall,

Is like the ten - der love of God For us made man-i - fest.
So we are pressed to bold - ly try To strive for dar - ing height.
Be - neath us lift God's might - y wings To bear us, one and all.

TEXT: R. Deane Postlethwaite (1925-1980), based on Deuteronomy 32:11

CAMPMEETING
CM

106   God of the Ages

1. God of the a - ges, his - to - ry's mak - er,
2. God of this morn - ing, glad - ly your chil - dren
3. God of to - mor - row, strong o - ver - com - er,
4. Lord of past a - ges, Lord of this morn - ing,

Plan-ning our path - way, hold-ing us fast,
Wor - ship be - fore you, trust-ing - ly bow:
Princ - es of dark - ness own your com - mand:
Lord of the fu - ture, help us, we pray:

Shap-ing in mer - cy all that con - cerns us:
Teach us to know you al - ways a - mong us,
What then can harm us? We are your peo - ple,
Teach us to trust you, love and o - bey you,

Fa - ther, we praise you, Lord of the past.
Qui - et - ly sov - 'reign— Lord of our now.
Now and for - ev - er kept by your hand.
Crown you each mo - ment, Lord of to - day.

TEXT: Margaret Clarkson
MUSIC: Traditional Gaelic Melody

BUNESSAN
10.9.10.9.

Christ Is Made the Sure Foundation 107

1. Christ is made the sure foun-da-tion, Christ, our head and
2. To this tem-ple where we call you, Come, O Lord of
3. Grant, we pray, to all your faith-ful All the gifts they
4. Praise and hon-or to the Fa-ther, Praise and hon-or

cor-ner-stone, Cho-sen of the Lord and pre-cious, Bind-ing
hosts, and stay; Come, with all your lov-ing-kind-ness, Hear your
ask to gain; What they gain from you for-ev-er With the
to the Son, Praise and hon-or to the Spir-it, Ev-er

all the Church in one; Ho-ly Zi-on's help for-ev-er
peo-ple as they pray; And your full-est ben-e-dic-tion
bless-ed to re-tain; And here-af-ter in your glo-ry
three and ev-er one: One in might and one in glo-ry

And our con-fi-dence a-lone.
Shed with-in these walls to-day.
Ev-er-more with you to reign.
While un-end-ing a-ges run! A-men.

TEXT: Latin hymn, 7th century; tr. John M. Neale
MUSIC: Dale Wood, arr. Marsha Foxgrover

EDEN CHURCH
8.7.8.7.8.7.

108 How Lovely on the Mountains
(Our God Reigns)

1. How love-ly on the moun-tains are the feet of him
2. It was our sin and guilt that bruised and wound-ed him.
3. Out of the tomb he came with grace and maj-es-ty;

who brings good news, good news;
It was our sin that brought him down.
he is a - live, he's a - live.

An-nounc-ing peace, pro-claim-ing news of hap-pi-ness,
When we like sheep had gone a-stray our Shep-herd came
God loves us so, see here his hands, his feet, his side

TEXT and MUSIC: Leonard E. Smith, Jr., based on Isaiah 52:7-10; arr. Roland Tabell
Copyright © 1974, 1978 Leonard E. Smith, Jr., New Jerusalem Music, P.O. Box 225, Clarksboro, N.J. 08020.

109   Joys Are Flowing Like a River
(Blessed Quietness)

1. Joys are flow - ing like a riv - er Since the
2. Bring-ing life and health and glad - ness All a -
3. Like the rain that falls from heav - en, Like the
4. See, a fruit - ful field is grow - ing, Bless - ed
5. What a won - der - ful sal - va - tion, Where we

Com - fort - er has come, Who a - bides with us for -
round, this heav'n-ly guest Ban-ished un - be - lief and
sun - light from the sky, So the Spir - it is now
fruit of right-eous - ness; And the streams of life are
al - ways see his face! What a per - fect hab - i -

ev - er, Makes the trust - ing heart his home.
sad - ness, Chang'd our wea - ri - ness to rest.
giv - en, Com - ing on us from on high.
flow - ing In the lone - ly wil - der - ness.
ta - tion, What a qui - et rest - ing place!

TEXT: Manie P. Ferguson
MUSIC: W. S. Marshall; arr. by James M. Kirk

BLESSED QUIETNESS
8.7.8.7. with refrain

Bless - ed qui - et - ness, ho - ly qui - et - ness— What as - sur - ance in my soul! On the storm - y sea he speaks peace to me— How the bil - lows cease to roll!

Thou Wilt Keep Them in Perfect Peace 110

Thou wilt keep them in per-fect peace Whose minds are stayed on thee. A - men.

TEXT: Isaiah 26:3
MUSIC: *Scottish Psalter,* 1615

DUKE'S TUNE
Irregular meter

111 Christ Is the World's Light

Unison

1. Christ is the world's light, Christ and none o - ther; Born in our dark - ness, he be - came our broth - er, If we have seen him, we have seen the Fa - ther:
2. Christ is the world's peace, Christ and none o - ther; No one can serve him and de - spise an - oth - er, Who else u - nites us one in God the Fa - ther?
3. Christ is the world's life, Christ and none o - ther; Sold once for sil - ver, mur - dered here, our broth - er, He who re - deems us reigns with God the Fa - ther.
4. Give God the glo - ry, God and none o - ther; Give God the glo - ry, Spir - it, Son, and Fa - ther; Give God the glo - ry, God with us my broth - er;

Glo - ry to God on high!

TEXT: Fred Pratt Green
MUSIC: From the *Paris Antiphoner*, 1746; harm. from *Westminster Praise* (Hinshaw, 1976)

CHRISTE SANCTORUM
10.11.11.6.

Christ Be My Leader

112

Unison

1. Christ be my lead-er by night as by day;
2. Christ be my teach-er in age as in youth,
3. Christ be my Sav-ior in calm as in strife;

Safe through the dark-ness, for Christ is the way.
Drift-ing or doubt-ing, for Christ is the truth.
Death can-not hold me for Christ is the life. Nor

Glad-ly I fol-low, my fu-ture his care,
Grant me to trust him; though shift-ing as sand,
dark-ness, nor doubt-ing, nor sin and its stain can

Dark-ness is day-light when Je-sus is there.
Doubt can-not daunt me; in Je-sus I stand.
Touch my sal-va-tion: with Je-sus I reign. A-men.

TEXT: Timothy Dudley-Smith
MUSIC: Traditional Irish Melody; harm. by Carlton R. Young

SLANE
10.10.10.10.

113   I Am the Bread of Life

1. I am the bread of life; _____ you who come to me shall not _____
(2.) bread that I will give _____ is my flesh for the life of the
(3.) less _____ you eat _____ of the flesh of the Son of _____
(4.) I am the res - ur - rec - tion, _____ I _____ am the _____
(5.) Lord, we be - lieve _____ that you _____ are the _____

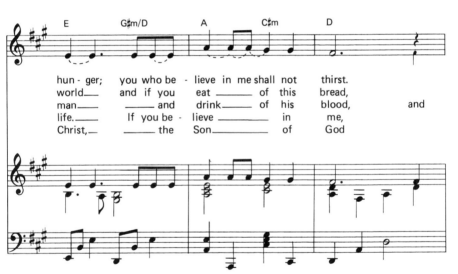

hun - ger; you who be - lieve in me shall not thirst.
world _____ and if you eat _____ of this bread,
man _____ _____ and drink _____ of his blood, and
life. _____ If you be - lieve _____ in me,
Christ, _____ _____ the Son _____ of God

TEXT and MUSIC: S. Suzanne Toolan; arr. Betty Pulkingham
Copyright © 1971, 1986 GIA Publications, Inc., Chicago, IL. All rights reserved.

No one can come to me____ un - less the____ Fa - ther beck - ons.
you shall____ live for - ev - er, you shall live for - ev - er.
drink____ of his blood____ you shall not have life with - in you.
ev - en____ tho' you die,____ you shall____ live for - ev - er.
who____ has come____ in - to____ the____ world.____

REFRAIN

And I will raise____ you up, and I will raise____ you

up,   and I will   raise_____ you   up____ on the

last_____   day.   day.

2. The
3. Un -
4. ——
5. Yes

Seek First the Kingdom

114

1. "Seek first the king - dom: 'tis your Fa - ther's will"—
2. As for hid - den trea - sure or for match-less pearl,
3. As the si - lent leav - en works its se - cret way,
4. As the ten - der seed - ling grows up tall and strong
5. Hum-blest shall be great - est, poor in spir - it reign;

So the voice of Je - sus bids us fol - low still.
When at last dis - cov - ered, some will sell their all;
Or as grows the seed grain through the night and day;
And the birds of heav - en to its branch-es throng,
Home shall come the child - like, born thro' thee a - gain;

Sav - ior, we would hear thee, fol - low, find, and see,
So, when breaks the vi - sion of that king - dom fair,
Lord, so be the in - crease peace - a - ble but sure,
So shall all God's chil - dren, from the east and west,
Ea - ger hearts ar - rive there on the pil - grim's road.

And in life's ad - ven - ture thy dis - ci - ples be.
Ours shall be its rich - es and its beau - ty rare.
Of thy word with - in us, and thy king - dom's pow'r.
Gath - er to his king - dom, in its shad - ow rest.
Hail! the king-dom glo - rious of the liv - ing God!

TEXT: Norman Elliott
MUSIC: Gustav Holst
Text © United Reformed Church

CRANHAM
11.11.11.11

115 He's Got the Whole World in His Hands

Unison

1. He's got the whole world in his hands, He's got the whole world in his hands, He's got the whole world in his hands, He's got the whole world in his hands.
2. He's got the wind and the rain in his hands, He's got the wind and the rain in his hands, He's got the wind and the rain in his hands, He's got the whole world in his hands.
3. He's got the ti-ny lit-tle ba-by in his hands, He's got the ti-ny lit-tle ba-by in his hands, He's got the ti-ny lit-tle ba-by in his hands, He's got the whole world in his hands.
4. He's got you and me, broth-er, in his hands, He's got you and me, sis-ter, in his hands, He's got you and me, broth-er, in his hands, He's got the whole world in his hands.

TEXT and MUSIC: Traditional spiritual; arr. by Eugene Thomas

SACRAMENTS

As We Gather at Your Table 116

1. As we gath-er at your ta-ble, As we lis-ten to your Word,
2. Turn our wor-ship in-to wit-ness In the sac-ra-ment of life;
3. Grant us vi-sion, gra-cious Spir-it, Seek-ing guests to share this feast

Help us know, O God, your pres-ence; Let our hearts and minds be stirred.
Send us forth to love and serve you, Bring-ing peace where there is strife.
Where tri-um-phant love will wel-come Those who had been last and least.

Nour-ish us with sa-cred sto-ry Till we claim it as our own;
Give us, Christ, your great com-pas-sion To for-give as you for-gave;
There no more will en-vy bind us Nor will pride our peace de-stroy,

Teach us through this ho-ly ban-quet How to make love's vic-t'ry known.
May we still be-hold your im-age In the world you died to save.
As we join with saints and an-gels To re-peat the sound-ing joy.

(Stanza 1 may be sung as preparation for communion, with stanzas 2 and 3 at its conclusion.)

TEXT: Carl P. Daw, Jr.
MUSIC: "The Sacred Harp"; harm. A. Royce Eckhardt

BEACH SPRING
8.7.8.7.D.

117 How Great the Joy

1. How great the joy the Lord pro-vides For us so free - ly here, When at his ta - ble he pre-sides And we to him draw near! His grace is new each day and hour, And we can rest up - on his pow'r.
2. It is so good to love the Lord, Who gave his life for all. So good to trust his liv - ing Word, Be lift - ed when we fall. When earth - ly plea - sures reach their end, Our feast of joy will just be - gin.
3. When shad - ows come, as come they will, And gloom per-vades the day, When hopes once bright grow cold and chill, The Lord pro-vides a way. In heav'n his light will al - ways shine, And bless - ed - ness be yours and mine.
4. So let us not be filled with care For home and dai - ly bread. In grace the Lord his love will share And sure - ly we'll be fed. Through all our days he's by our side, He bears what-ev - er may be - tide.
5. With joy we walk with Je - sus here, How great a friend is he! But think what joy a - waits us there, When heav - en's light we see. Our hopes and dreams will be com - plete, When at the heav'n - ly feast we meet. Hal -

REFRAIN

TEXT: Nils Frykman; tr. Aaron Markuson, Glen V. Wiberg
MUSIC: "Engelke's Lofsånger"
Words copyright © 1978 by Covenant Publications.

DAY OF REDEMPTION
8.6.8.6.8.8. with Refrain

At the Lamb's High Feast 118

Unison

1. At the Lamb's high feast we sing Praise to
2. Praise we him, whose love di - vine Gives his
3. Where the pas - chal blood is poured Death's dread
4. Praise we Christ, whose blood was shed, Pas - chal

our vic - tor - ious king, Who has washed us
sa - cred blood for wine, Gives his bod - y
an - gel sheathes the sword; Is - rael's hosts tri -
vic - tim, pas - chal bread; With sin - cer - i -

in the tide Flow - ing from his pierc - ed side, Al - le - lu - ia!
for the feast— Christ the vic - tim, Christ the priest. Al - le - lu - ia!
um-phant go Through the wave that drowns the foe. Al - le - lu - ia!
ty and love Eat we man - na from a - bove. Al - le - lu - ia!

TEXT: Office Hymn, 17th Century; tr. Robert Campbell
MUSIC: Bohemian Brethren, Kirkegesang, 1566
Arr. copyright 1969 Concordia Publishing House. Reprinted by permission.

SONNE DER GERECHTIGKEIT
7.7.7.7.4.

119

Come, Let Us Eat

(2-part canon)

I Men

II Women and children echo throughout

1. Come, let us eat for now the feast is spread.
2. Come, let us drink for now the wine is poured.
3. In the Lord's pres-ence now we meet and rest.
4. Rise, then, to spread a - broad God's might - y Word.

Come, let us eat for now the feast is spread.
Come, let us drink for now the wine is poured.
In the Lord's pres-ence now we meet and rest.
Rise, then, to spread a - broad God's might - y Word.

Our Lord's bod - y, let us take to - geth - er.
Je - sus' blood poured, let us drink to - geth - er.
In the pres - ence of our Lord we gath - er.
Je - sus ris - en will bring in the king-dom.

+ *African drums:*

TEXT: Billema Kwillia, Sts. 1-3; Gilbert E. Doan, St. 4, alt.;
Tr. Margaret D. Miller Sts. 1-3, alt.
MUSIC: Billema Kwillia; arr. by Roland Tabell
Text copyright by Lutheran World Federation, Sts. 1-3. Used by permission.
Copyright 1972 Contemporary Worship 4: Hymns for Baptism and Holy Communion, St. 4.
Reprinted by permission of Augsburg Fortress. Tune copyright by Lutheran World Federation. Used by permission.

Our Lord's bod-y, let us take to - geth-er.
Je - sus' blood poured, let us drink to - geth-er.
In the pres - ence of our Lord we gath-er.
Je - sus ris - en will bring in the king-dom.

Eat This Bread

120

Eat this bread, drink this cup, come to me and
nev - er be hun - gry. Eat this bread, drink this cup,
trust in me and you will not thirst.

WORDS: Robert Batastini and the Taizé Community, 1982 (Jn. 6:35)
MUSIC: Jacques Berthier, 1982
© 1984 Les Presses de Taizé France; by permission of G. I. A. Publications, Inc.

BERTHIER
Irr.

121 · In the Breaking of Bread

In the break - ing of bread and the pass - ing of
In the break - ing of bread and the pass - ing of

wine We know you are here, Lord Je -
wine We know you are here, Lord Je -

sus, Just as on the day you met on the
sus, Your words pierce our grief with hope and re -

way Two friends who re - ceived you in._____
lief From an - guish of dark - er hours._____

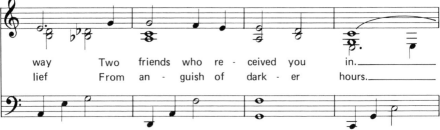

TEXT and MUSIC: Richard K. Carlson
Copyright © 1989 Richard K. Carlson. Used with permission.

Our sins we con-fess, with these gifts that you
Our hearts burn in-side, and our eyes o-pen

bless, For we know, Lord, that you are here.
wide, For we know, Lord, that you are here.

Jesus, Remember Me 122

Je-sus, re-mem-ber me when you come in-to your king-dom.

Je-sus, re-mem-ber me when you come in-to your king-dom.

End of medley from 130

TEXT: Luke 23:42
MUSIC: Jacques Berthier and the Community of Taizé, 1981
Music © 1981 Les Presses de Taizé, by permission of G.I.A. Publications, Inc.

REMEMBER ME
Irr.

123 You Satisfy the Hungry Heart
(Gift of Finest Wheat)

REFRAIN

You sat-is-fy the hun-gry heart With gift of fin-est wheat; Come give to us, O sav-ing Lord, The bread of life to eat.

Fine

1. As when the shep - herd calls his sheep, They
2. With joy - ful lips we sing to you Our
3. Is not the cup we bless and share The
4. The mys - t'ry of your pres - ence, Lord, No
5. You give your - self to us, O Lord; Then

WORDS: Omer Westendorf
MUSIC: Robert E. Krentz

FINEST WHEAT
CMD with Refrain

Jesus Calls Us to His Feast 124

TEXT: James Lindgren
MUSIC: Ronald Coleman; arr. Betty Jo MacPhee
Text copyright James Lindgren; music copyright Ronald Coleman. Used by permission.

125 In Celebration, Clap Your Hands and Sing
(Celebration Unending)

Unison

1. In cel - e - bra - tion, clap your hands and sing In
2. We drink the wine, to - geth - er break the bread— Each
3. With joy we go to take our place each day, Liv -
4. Past place and time, we rise be - yond this earth— Our

praise to God, our ev - er - liv - ing king; With
one in turn is com - fort - ed and fed; We
Liv - ing our lives by fol - low - ing Christ's way; In
fel - low - ship in heav - en finds re - birth; A -

joy - ful hearts our wor - ship now we bring:
join our hands— one bod - y, Christ the head:
all we do, we sing, we serve, we pray:
new our voic - es sing the Sav - ior's worth:

TEXT: Carol Fox Thorne, Stanzas 1, 2, and 4; Paul H. Erickson, Stanza 3
MUSIC: Ralph Vaughan Williams
Words Stanzas 1, 2, and 4 copyright © 1982 by Christianity Today. Used by permission.
Stanza 3 copyright © 1990 by Covenant Publications.
Music from The English Hymnal *by permission of Oxford University Press.*

SINE NOMINE
10.10.10. with alleluias

Al - le - lu - ia! Al - le - lu - ia! A-men.

Now Let Us from This Table Rise 126

Unison

1. Now let us from this ta - ble rise, Re - newed in bod - y,
2. With minds a - lert, up - held by grace, To spread the Word in
3. To fill each hu - man house with love, It is the sac - ra -
4. Then grant us cou - rage, gra - cious God, To choose a - gain the

mind, and soul; With Christ we die and live a - gain, His
speech and deed, We fol - low in the steps of Christ, At
ment of care; The work that Christ be - gan to do We
pil - grim way; And help us to ac - cept with joy The

self - less love has made us whole.
one with all in hope and need.
hum - bly pledge our - selves to share.
chal - lenge of to - mor - row's day. A - men.

TEXT: Fred Kaan
MUSIC: Thoman Tallis

TALLIS' CANON
L.M.

127 Water of Life
(2-part canon)

TEXT and MUSIC: David Haas; arr. Roland Tabell

light; Jour - ney from death to new life.

Jour - ney from death to new life.

I Come with Joy

128

Unison

1. I come with joy to meet my Lord, for - giv - en,
2. I come with Chris - tians far and near to find, as
3. As Christ breaks bread and bids us share, each proud di -
4. And thus with joy we meet our Lord. his pres - ence,
5. To - geth - er met, to - geth - er bound, we'll go our

loved, and free, In awe and won - der to re - call his
all are fed, The new com-mun - i - ty of love in
vi - sion ends. The love that made us, makes us one, and
al - ways near, Is in such friend-ship bet - ter known; we
dif - f'rent ways, And as his peo - ple in the world, we'll

life laid down for me, his life laid down for me.
Christ's com-mun -ion bread, in Christ's com-mun - ion bread.
stran - gers now are friends, and stran - gers now are friends.
see and praise him here; we see and praise him here.
live and speak his praise, we'll live and speak his praise.

WORDS: Brian Wren
MUSIC: American Folk Tune; arr. by Austin C. Lovelace

DOVE OF PEACE
CM

129 When John Baptized by Jordan's River

With spirit

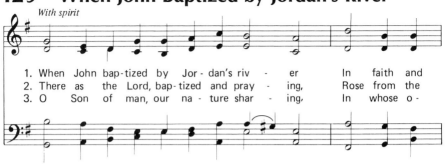

1. When John bap-tized by Jor-dan's riv - er   In   faith and
2. There as   the Lord, bap-tized and pray - ing,   Rose from the
3. O   Son of man, our na - ture shar - ing,   In whose o -

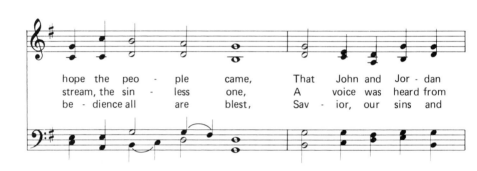

hope the peo - ple   came,   That John and Jor - dan
stream, the sin - less   one,   A   voice was heard from
be - dience all   are   blest,   Sav - ior, our sins and

might de - liv - er   Their trou-bled souls from sin and shame.
heav - en say - ing,   "This is   my own be - lov - ed Son."
sor - rows bear - ing, Hear us and grant us this re - quest:

TEXT: Timothy Dudley Smith
MUSIC: from Genevan Psalter, harm. Dale Grotenhuis
Text copyright 1984 by Hope Publishing Company, Carol Stream, IL 60188.
Harm. copyright © 1987, CRC Publications, Grand Rapids, MI 49560.
All rights reserved. Used by permission.

RENDEZ A DIEU
9.8.9.8.D

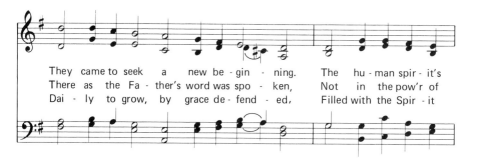

They came to seek a new be - gin - ning. The hu - man spir - it's
There as the Fa - ther's word was spo - ken, Not in the pow'r of
Dai - ly to grow, by grace de - fend - ed, Filled with the Spir - it

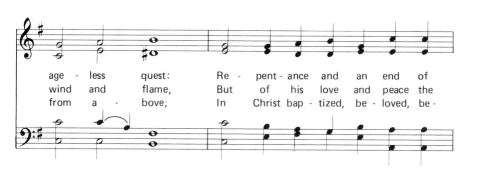

age - less quest: Re - pent - ance and an end of
wind and flame, But of his love and peace the
from a - bove; In Christ bap - tized, be - loved, be -

sin - ning, Re - nounc - ing ev - 'ry wrong con - fessed.
to - ken, Seen as a dove, the Spir - it came.
friend - ed, Chil - dren of God in peace and love.

The hymnbook reflects the history of the Church, embodies the
doctrine of the Church, expresses the devotional feeling of the
Church, and demonstrates the unity of the Church.

W.M. Taylor

130   O How He Loves You and Me!

1. O how he loves you and me.
2. Je-sus to Cal-v'ry did go,

O how he loves you and me;
Love for all peo-ple to show;

He gave his life, what more could he give?
What he did there brought hope from de-spair:

O how he loves you; O how he loves me;
O how he loves you; O how he loves me;

O how he loves you and me!
O how he loves you and me!

TEXT and MUSIC: Kurt Kaiser

Medley option: 130,122

PATRICIA
Irregular meter

WITNESS

If It Had Not Been for the Lord 131

TEXT and MUSIC: Margaret Pleasant Douroux

132 **Give Me Jesus**

1. In the morn-ing when I rise, In the morn-ing when I
2. Dark mid-night was my cry, Dark mid-night was my
3. Just a-bout the break of day, Just a-bout the break of
4. Oh, when I come to die, Oh, when I come to

rise, In the morn-ing when I rise, Give me Je - sus.
cry, Dark mid-night was my cry, Give me Je - sus.
day, Just a-bout the break of day, Give me Je - sus.
die, Oh, when I come to die, Give me Je - sus.

REFRAIN

Give me Je - sus, Give me Je - sus,

You may have all the rest, Give me Je - sus.

TEXT and MUSIC: Afro-American Spiritual; arr. by Alma Blackmon
Arrangement copyright © 1984 by Alma Blackmon.

O How Blest to Be a Pilgrim

133

1. O how blest to be a pil - grim, Guid - ed by the Fa - ther's hand;
2. On this side of Jor - dan's riv - er, Sights too deep for words are known,
3. There no clouds of dark - ness gath - er, Neith-er sor - row, tears, nor woe,
4. Here from loved ones we are part - ed, Earth - ly sor - rows nev - er cease,
5. O may none give up the jour - ney, Left in dark - ness on the shore,

Free at last from ev - 'ry bur - den We shall en - ter Ca - naan's land.
But we look for bright to - mor - rows In Je - ru - sa - lem our home.
Noth-ing harm-ful e'er shall en - ter, Sin and pain we will not know.
But with - in that glo - rious cit - y We shall meet a - gain in peace.
May we all at last be gath - ered When our pil - grim - age is o'er.

REFRAIN

Songs of vic - t'ry there shall greet us, Like the thun-d'ring of a might-y

flood. End-less prais-es be to Je - sus, Who re-deemed us by his blood!

TEXT: Joel Blomquist and Lars P. Ollén; tr. Signe L. Bennett and Glen V. Wiberg
MUSIC: Robert Lowry; harm. Kenneth L. Fenton
Words copyright © 1978 by Covenant Publications

HANSON PLACE
8.7.8.7. with refrain

134 Love Divine, So Great and Wondrous!
(He the Pearly Gates Will Open)

1. Love di-vine so great and won - drous! Deep and might-y, pure, sub-lime!
2. Like a dove when hunt-ed, fright - ened, As a wound-ed fawn was I;
3. Love di-vine, so great and won - drous! All my sin he then for - gave!
4. In life's e - ven-tide, at twi - light, At his door, I'll knock and wait;

Com - ing from the heart of Je - sus—Just the same thro' tests of time.
Bro - ken-heart-ed, yet he healed me— He will heed the sin - ner's cry.
I will sing his praise for - ev - er, For his blood, his pow'r to save.
By the pre - cious love of Je - sus I shall en - ter heav - en's gate.

He the pearl - y gates will o - pen, So that I may en-ter in;

For he pur-chased my re - demp -tion And for - gave me all my sin.

TEXT: Fredrik A. Blom; tr. Nathaniel Carlson
MUSIC: Alfred Olsen-Dulin, Arr. Norman Johnson

Medley option: 134,135

ETERNAL DESTINY
8.7.8.7. with refrain

Sing the Wondrous Love of Jesus

(When We All Get to Heaven)

135

1. Sing the won-drous love of Je-sus, Sing his mer-cy and his grace;
2. While we walk the pil-grim path-way Clouds will o-ver-spread the sky;
3. Let us then be true and faith-ful, Trust-ing, serv-ing ev-'ry day;
4. On-ward to the prize be-fore us! Soon his beau-ty we'll be-hold;

In the man-sions bright and bless-ed He'll pre-pare for us a place.
But when trav-'ling days are o-ver Not a shad-ow, not a sigh.
Just one glimpse of him in glo-ry Will the toils of life re-pay.
Soon the pearl-y gates will o-pen— We shall tread the streets of gold.

CHORUS

When we all get to heav-en, What a day of re-joic-ing that will be! When we all see Je-sus, We'll sing and shout the vic-to-ry.

When we all ... What a ... day of re-joic-ing that will be! When we all ... shout, and shout the vic-to-ry.

End of medley

TEXT: Eliza E. Hewitt
MUSIC: Emily D. Wilson

HEAVEN
8.7.8.7. with refrain

136

When I Remember
(Cuando Recuerdo)

Lively

When I re-mem-ber that he died for me, I ne-ver can go back a-gain. Al-le-lu-ia! When I re-mem-ber that he died for me, I ne-ver can go back a-gain. No! No! No! No! No! I ne-ver can go back a-gain. Al-le-lu-ia! No! No! No! No! No! I ne-ver can go back a-gain.

TEXT and MUSIC: Traditional Mexican

Who Can Cheer the Heart Like Jesus?   137
(All That Thrills My Soul)

1. Who can cheer the heart like Je - sus, / By his pres-ence all di - vine?
2. Love of Christ so free-ly giv - en, / Grace of God be-yond de - gree.
3. What a won-der-ful re - demp - tion! / Nev - er can a mor-tal know
4. Ev - 'ry need his hand sup - ply - ing, / Ev - 'ry good in him I see;
5. By the crys-tal flow-ing riv - er / With the ran-somed I will sing.

True and ten-der, pure and pre - cious, / O how blest to call him mine!
Mer - cy high-er than the heav - en, / Deep-er than the deep-est sea!
How my sin, though red like crim - son, / Can be whit - er than the snow.
On his strength di-vine re - ly - ing, / He is all in all to me.
And for - ev - er and for - ev - er / Praise and glo-ri-fy the King.

REFRAIN

All that thrills my soul is Je - sus, He is more than life to me; to me;

And the fair - est of ten thou - sand In my bless-ed Lord I see.

TEXT and MUSIC: Thoro Harris
Copyright 1931. Renewed 1959 by Nazarene Publishing House. Used by permission.
HARRIS
8.7.8.7. with refrain

138

God Sent His Son
(Because He Lives)

1. God sent his Son, they called him Je - sus; He came to love, heal, and for - give; He lived and died to buy my par - don, An emp-ty grave is there to prove my Sav-ior lives.

2. And then one day I'll cross the riv - er; I'll fight life's fi - nal war with pain; And then as death gives way to vic - t'ry, I'll see the lights of glo - ry and I'll know he lives.

Be-cause he lives I can face to - mor-row; Be-cause he lives all fear is gone; Be-cause I know he holds the

TEXT: Gloria and William J. Gaither
MUSIC: William J. Gaither

RESURRECTION
Irregular

fu - ture.   And life   is   worth the liv-ing   just be-cause he lives.

How I Love You
(You Are the One)

139

| G | D | Em | Bm | C | G |

1. How   love   you,_____   you are the one._____
2. I   was   so   lost,   but you showed the way,   'cause
3. I   was   lied   to,   but you told the truth,   'cause
4. I   was   dy - ing,   but you gave me life,   'cause

| Am | Bm/D | D | G | D | Em | Bm |

you are the one!   How   love   you,_____
you are the way.   I   was   so   lost,   but
you are the truth.   I   was   lied   to,   but
you are the life.   I   was   dy - ing,   and

| C | G | D | [1,2,3] G | | [4] G |

you are the one   for   me.
you showed the way   to   me.
you showed the truth   to   me.
you gave your life   for   me.

TEXT and MUSIC: Keith Green. Based on John 14:6.

140 When Peace, Like a River
(It Is Well with My Soul)

1. When peace, like a riv-er, at-tend-eth my way, When
2. Though Sa-tan should buf-fet, tho' tri-als should come, Let
3. My sin— O, the bliss of this glo-ri-ous thought, My
4. And, Lord, haste the day when the faith shall be sight, The

sor-rows like sea-bil-lows roll; What-ev-er my
this blest as-sur-ance con-trol, That Christ has re-
sin— not in part, but the whole, Is nailed to the
clouds be rolled back as a scroll, The trum-pet shall

lot, thou hast taught me to say, "It is well, it is
gard-ed my help-less es-tate, And hath shed his own
cross, and I bear it no more, Praise the Lord, praise the
sound and the Lord shall de-scend, e-ven so— it is

REFRAIN

well with my soul." It is well, with my
blood for my soul. It is well
Lord, O my soul!
well with my soul.

TEXT: Horatio G. Spafford
MUSIC: Philip P. Bliss

VILLE DU HAVRE
11.8.11.9. with Refrain

soul, with my soul, It is well, it is well with my soul.

Is It True? 141

1. Is it true that Je - sus is my broth - er? Is it
2. He's my broth - er! won - der of all won - ders; Great - er
3. Je - sus said, "My fa - ther is your fa - ther," And he
4. So I go re - joic - ing in the fu - ture, For the

true joint heir I am to be? O how can I then be ev - er
grace God nev - er could be - stow, Tho' I can - not ful - ly un - der
said, "My God is your God, too;" O my soul can-not with-hold re-
things God has pre - pared for me, Ev - er - last - ing life with joy un-

anx - ious O'er the things this earth may hold for me.
stand it By his Word this bless - ed truth I know.
joic - ing, For this I know, his words are al - ways true.
end - ing, Ev - er in his pres - ence I shall be.

TEXT: Lina Sandell; tr. Walter Johnson
MUSIC: Oscar Ahnfelt

BROTHER
10.9.10.9

142

Tell Out, My Soul

TEXT: Timothy Dudley-Smith, Luke 1:46-55
MUSIC: Walter Greatorex, alt.

WOODLANDS
10.10.10.10.

prom - ise of his Word; In God my
age to age the same; His ho - ly
wills are put to flight, The hun - gry
great - ness of the Lord To chil - dren's

Sav - ior shall my heart re - joice.
name, the Lord, the might - y one.
fed, the hum - ble lift - ed high.
chil - dren and for - ev - er - more!

Sing, therefore, you Christians. Rekindle that sacred glow in your
souls at the holy altar of song. Sing peace into your own hearts.
Sing the doubting and hesitating ones into the presence of
Christ. While we are still on this earth our song should continually grow stronger, more joyful, and more rich in meaning. If thus
we sing here and now, our song before the throne of God when
we have entered into "life more abundant" will be doubly
glorious. The Lord entrusts sacred song to human lips. It is a
God-given privilege to sing with gladness of heart, as a beautiful
testimony to our Christian faith and devotion.

Oscar Lövgren

143   I'm So Glad, Jesus Lifted Me

1. I'm so glad,
2. Sa-tan had me bound,
3. When I was in trou-ble,

Je-sus lift-ed me,

I'm so glad,
Sa-tan had me bound,
When I was in trou-ble,

Je-sus lift-ed me,

I'm so glad,
Sa-tan had me bound,
When I was in trou-ble,

Je-sus lift-ed me, Sing-ing

TEXT and MUSIC: Afro-American spiritual. Harm. by Richard Smallwood.
Copyright © 1977 Richwood Music

glo - ry, hal - le - lu - jah!   Je - sus lift - ed me.

SING ALL. See that you join with the congregation as frequently as you can. Let not a slight degree of weakness or weariness hinder you. If it is a cross to you, take it up, and you will find it a blessing.

SING LUSTILY, and with good courage. Beware of singing as if you are half-dead or half-asleep; but lift up your voice with strength. Be no more afraid of your voice now, nor more ashamed of its being heard, than when you sing the songs of Satan.

SING MODESTLY. Do not bawl, so as to be heard above or distinct from the rest of the congregation—that you may not destroy the harmony—but strive to unite your voices together so as to make one clear melodious sound.

SING IN TIME. Whatever time is sung, be sure to keep up with it. Do not run before nor stay behind it; but attend close to the leading voices, and move therewith as exactly as you can; and take care not to sing *too slow*. This drawling way naturally steals in on all who are lazy; and it is high time to drive it out from among us, and sing all our tunes as quick as we did at first.

ABOVE ALL SING SPIRITUALLY. Have an eye to God in every word you sing. Aim at pleasing him more than yourself, or any other creature. In order to do this, attend strictly to the sense of what you sing, and see that your heart is not carried away with the sound, but offered to God continually; so shall your singing be such as the Lord will approve of here, and reward you when he comes in the clouds of heaven.

John Wesley, "Directions for Singing"

144   Soon and Very Soon

Rhythmically

1, 4. Soon and ve - ry soon   we are going to see the King.
2. No more cry - ing there,
3. No more dy - ing there,

Soon and ve - ry soon   we are going to
No more cry - ing there,
No more dy - ing there,

see the King.   Soon and ve - ry soon   we are
No more cry-ing there,
No more dy- ing there,

going to see the King.   Hal-le - lu - jah, Hal-le - lu - jah, we're

TEXT and MUSIC: Andráe Crouch
*Copyright 1978, Communique' Music (Admin. by Copyright Management,
Inc.) Crouch Music.*

going to see the King. Hal - le -
lu - jah, Hal - le - lu - jah, we're going to see the King.

After this I looked, and there was an enormous crowd—no one could count all the people! They were from every race, tribe, nation, and language, and they stood in front of the throne and of the Lamb, dressed in white robes and holding palm branches in their hands. They called out in a loud voice: "Salvation comes from our God, who sits on the throne, and from the Lamb!" All the angels stood around the throne, the elders, and the four living creatures. Then they threw themselves face downward in front of the throne and worshiped God, saying, "Amen! Praise, glory, wisdom, thanksgiving, honor, power, and might belong to our God forever and ever! Amen!"

One of the elders asked me, "Who are these people dressed in white robes, and where do they come from?"

"I don't know, sir. You do," I answered him.

He said to me, "These are the people who have come up safely through the terrible persecution. They have washed their robes and made them white with the blood of the Lamb. That is why they stand before God's throne and serve him day and night in his temple. He who sits on the throne will protect them with his presence. Never again will they hunger or thirst; neither sun nor any scorching heat will burn them, because the Lamb, who is in the center of the throne, will be their shepherd, and he will guide them to springs of life-giving water. And God will wipe away every tear from their eyes."

Revelation 7:9-17, *TEV*

145   You Have Turned Our Sadness
(Psalm 30)

You have turned our sad - ness in -
(my)

to a joy - ful dance, you are our Lord, our
(my)

God.   God.

TEXT: Psalm 30:11a; adapted by Elise S. Eslinger
MUSIC: Elise S. Eslinger

Text adapted from Good News Bible, *The Bible in Today's English Version* © *American Bible Society, 1966, 1971, 1976.*
Adaptation from The Upper Room Worshipbook © *1984 by The Upper Room, Nashville.*
Music from The Upper Room Worshipbook © *1985 by The Upper Room, Nashville.*

I.*   Lord, I exalt you, for you lift me up,
       And keep my foes from rejoicing over me.
    My God, I cry to you for help;
       It is you who heal me, Lord.
    You brought me up from the grave;
       You restored me to life from among the dead.

II.   Let faithful people sing to the Lord;
       Let them praise the holy God,
    Whose anger is brief, whose grace is lifelong—
       We weep in the evening, but laugh at dawn.   REFRAIN

I.   I, unconcerned, said to myself,
       "I will never stumble."
    You allowed me to stand like a splendid mountain;
       But you hid your face, and I was in terror.

II.   I cried out to you, Lord;
       I sought my Lord's mercy—
    "What will you gain if I die in tears?
       Does dust declare your faithful love?"

I+II.   Lord, you heard, and were gracious to me;
       O Lord, you were my helper.
    You turned my grief into dancing,
       Stripped me of sorrow and clothed me with joy.
    So my heart will sing to you, not weep;
       Lord, my God, I will praise you forever.   REFRAIN

*I and II may be read by 2 leaders; leader/congregation; male/female; 2 sides of group, etc.

Verse translation from *The Psalms: A New Translation for Prayer and Worship,* by Gary Chamberlain,
© 1989 by The Upper Room, Nashville.

146 As the Music to the Singer

1. As the mu-sic to the sing-er, As one's thought to spo-ken word.
4. Bound to him and by him hold-en, As the flute and breath ac-cord.

Fine

As the rose to fra-grant o-dor, So to me is Christ the Lord.
His for now and His for-ev-er, Is my soul to Christ the Lord.

2. As the moth-er to her ba-by, As the trav-'ler to the guide,
3. As the sun to glad-'ning day-spring, As the oil is to the flame.

D.C. al Fine

As the lake to stream-ing rain-fall Stands the Sav-ior by my side.
As the fish is to the wa-ter, So to me is his sweet name.

D.C. al Fine

TEXT: Narayan Vaman Tilak; tr. by Nicol Macnicol
MUSIC: Chinese melody; arr. Marsha Foxgrover and Roland Tabell
Translation used by permission of the Trustees of the late Miss Helen M. Macnicol.
Arr. copyright 1990 by Covenant Publications.

Orff instruments may be used with the first two lines on previous page.

My Soul Gives Glory to My God   147
(Magnificat)

1. My soul gives glo - ry to my God. My
2. My God has done great things for me:
3. From age to age, to all who fear, Such
4. Love casts the might - y from their thrones, Pro -
5. Praise God, whose lov - ing cov - e - nant Sup -

heart pours out its praise. God lift - ed up my
Ho - ly is God's name. All peo - ple will de -
mer - cy love im - parts. Dis - pens - ing jus - tice
motes the in - se - cure, Leaves hun - gry spir - its
ports those in dis - tress, Re - mem - ber - ing past

low - li - ness In man - y mar - vel-ous ways.
clare me blessed, And bless - ings they shall claim.
far and near, Dis - miss - ing self - ish hearts.
sat - is - fied, The rich seem sud-den-ly poor.
prom - is - es With pres - ent faith - ful - ness.

TEXT: Sister Miriam Therese Winter, based on Luke 1:46-55
MUSIC: Melody from Wyeth's Repository of Sacred Music; harm. A. Royce Eckhardt.
Text copyright © Medical Mission Sisters, 1978, 1987. Reproduced with permission of copyright owner.
Harm. copyright © 1989 A. Royce Eckhardt.

RESPONSE

Come to the Savior, Make No Delay 148

1. Come to the Sav-ior, make no de-lay; Here in his Word he's shown us the way;
2. "Suf - fer the chil-dren!" O hear his voice, Let ev-'ry heart leap forth and re-joice,
3. Think once a-gain, he's with us to-day; Heed now his blest com-mands, and o-bey;

Here in our midst he's stand-ing to-day, Ten-der-ly say-ing, "Come!"
And let us free-ly make him our choice; Do not de-lay, but come.
Hear now his ac - cents ten - der-ly say, "Will you, my chil-dren, come?"

REFRAIN

Joy-ful, joy - ful will the meet-ing be, When from sin our hearts are pure and free;

And we shall gath-er, Sav-ior, with thee, In our e-ter-nal home.

TEXT and MUSIC: George Frederick Root

COME TO THE SAVIOR
9.9.9.6. with Refrain

149   Do You Live?
(Lever du?)

1. Do you live the life that's giv - en   Thro' your faith in Christ, the Lord?
2. Pray that Je-sus may a - wak - en   Spir - it - life for - ev - er new!
3. Do I seek the Sav-ior's glo - ry?   In his fear am I con-tent?
4. Be my life, as well, in dy - ing—   Death will some day come to me—

Is your name in-scribed in heav - en   In the king-dom of our Lord?
Pray that sin may be for - sak - en   Which breeds on-ly death in you!
Is his Ho - ly Spir - it near me   And his Word my nour-ish-ment?
Grant that in my last pri - va - tion   I may still en-liv-ened be,

Do you live the life that's new?   Tell me true.
Ask your-self each day he gives,   Do I live?
O Lord Je - sus, come and be   Life in me.
And un - end-ing - ly a - bide   By your side.

Do you live the life that's new?   Tell me true.
Ask your-self each day he gives,   Do I live?
O, Lord Je - sus, come and be   Life in me.
And un - end-ing - ly a - bide   By your side.

TEXT: Lina Sandell; tr. Karl A. Olsson, dedicated to the memory of A. Eldon Palmquist.
MUSIC: Swedish melody
Copyright © 1989 Covenant Publications

Now, Anxious Heart
Awake from Your Sadness

150

1. Now, an-xious heart, a - wake from your sad - ness, Have you for-
got - ten the things that re - main; Grace and com-mun - ion,
Un - bro - ken un - ion With Christ a - ris - en and ev - er the same?

2. Is God not still your heav - en - ly Fa - ther, Has Je - sus
changed since he suf - fered and died? Is not the Spir - it,
plead - ing and lead - ing, Ev - er the coun-sel-or, help-er, and guide?

3. Are not the saints a tri - fle con - fus - ing, They speak of
joy but great tri - als en - dure, King - doms pos-sess - ing,
plead - ing a bless - ing, Safe in God's keep-ing but ne - ver se - cure?

4. See - ing by faith what's hid - den to vi - sion This is the
rule in the king - dom di - vine, Mo - ments of feel - ing,
of - ten con-ceal - ing That which in truth we pos - sess all the time.

5. So, anx-ious heart, a - wake from your sad - ness, Rise to re-
mem - ber your bless - ings to claim. Though skies be cloud - ed
and the sun shroud - ed, Nev - er for-get it is there just the same.

TEXT: Carl Olof Rosenius, tr. Herbert E. Palmquist
MUSIC: Oscar Ahnfelt, harm. A. Royce Eckhardt

ANXIOUS HEART
10.10.10.10.

151 **I, the Lord of Sea and Sky**

(Here I Am, Lord)

1. I, the Lord of sea and sky, I have heard my peo-ple cry.
2. I, the Lord of snow and rain, I have borne my peo-ple's pain.
3. I, the Lord of wind and flame, I will tend the poor and lame.

All who dwell in dark and sin My hand will save.
I have wept for love of them, They turn a - way.
I will set a feast for them, My hand will save.

I who made the stars of night, I will make their
I will break their hearts of stone, Give them hearts for
Fin-est bread I will pro-vide Till their hearts be

dark - ness bright. Who will bear my light to them? Whom shall I
love a - lone. I will speak my word to them. Whom shall I
sat - is - fied. I will give my life to them. Whom shall I

TEXT: Isaiah 6; Daniel I. Schutte and North American Liturgy Resources
MUSIC: Dan Schutte, SJ, Harm. by Michael Pope, SJ, Dan Schutte, SJ, and John Weissrock
Copyright © 1981 by Daniel Schutte and NALR, Phoenix, AZ 85029.

152   Softly and Tenderly Jesus Is Calling

1. Soft - ly and ten - der - ly Je - sus is call - ing,
2. Why should we tar - ry when Je - sus is plead - ing,
3. Time is now fleet - ing, the mo - ments are pass - ing,
4. O for the won - der - ful love he has prom - ised,

Call - ing for you and for me; See, on the
Plead- ing for you and for me? Why should we
Pass - ing from you and from me; Shad - ows are
Prom-ised for you and for me; Though we have

por - tals he's wait - ing and watch - ing, Watch - ing for
lin - ger and heed not his mer - cies, Mer - cies for
gath - er - ing, death soon is com - ing, Com - ing for
sinned he has mer - cy and par - don, Par - don for

you and for me.
you and for me? Come home, come home,
you and for me. Come home, come home,
you and for me.

TEXT and MUSIC: Will L. Thompson

THOMPSON
11.7.11.7. with refrain

You who are wea-ry, come home; Ear-nest-ly, ten-der-ly,

Je-sus is call-ing— Call-ing, "O sin-ner, come home!"

Happy Those Who Hear God's Word 153
(4-part canon)

I   II

Hap - py those who hear God's Word. Hap - py those who keep God's Word.

III   IV

Al - le - lu - ia, Al - le - lu - ia, Al - le - lu - ia.

TEXT and MUSIC: Jack Miffleton
Copyright © 1983 North American Liturgy Resources, 10802 N. 23rd Ave., Phoenix, Arizona 85029.
All rights reserved. Used with permission.

154   I Was There to Hear Your Borning Cry

1. +7. I was there to hear your born - ing cry, I'll be
3. When you heard the won - der of the Word I was
5. In the mid - dle a - ges of your life, Not too

there when you are old. I re - joiced the day you
there to cheer you on; You were raised to praise the
old, no long - er young, I'll be there to guide you

were bap - tized, To see your life un - fold.
liv - ing Lord, To whom you now be - long.
through the night, Com - plete what I've be - gun.

2. I was there when you were but a child, With a
4. When you find some - one to share your time And you
6. When the eve - ning gent - ly clos - es in And you

faith to suit you well; In a blaze of light you
join your hearts as one, I'll be there to make your
shut your wea - ry eyes, I'll be there as I have

wan - dered off to find where de - mons dwell.
vers - es rhyme from dusk till ris - ing sun.
al - ways been with just one more sur - prise.

Jesus Is Born!   155
(4-part canon)

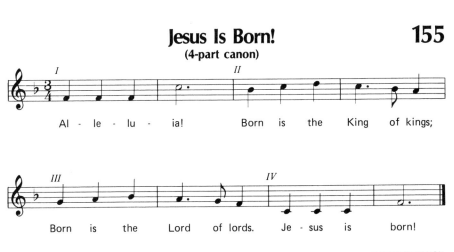

Al - le - lu - ia! Born is the King of kings;

Born is the Lord of lords. Je - sus is born!

TEXT and MUSIC: Gerald S. Henderson
Copyright © 1986 WORD MUSIC (a div. of WORD, INC.). All rights reserved.
International copyright secured. Used by permission.

NATIVITY CANON
4.6.6.4.

156   I Want to Walk As a Child of the Light

Richly

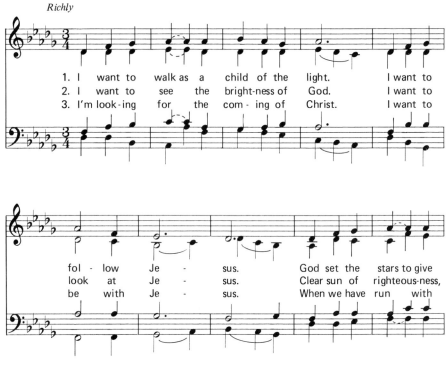

1. I want to walk as a child of the light. I want to
2. I want to see the bright-ness of God. I want to
3. I'm look-ing for the com-ing of Christ. I want to

fol - low Je - sus. God set the stars to give
look at Je - sus. Clear sun of righteous-ness,
be with Je - sus. When we have run with

light to the world. The star of my life is Je - sus.
shine on my path, and show me the way to the Fa - ther.
pa-tience the race, we shall know the joy of Je - sus.

TEXT and MUSIC: Kathleen Thomerson

In him there is no dark - ness at all, the night and the day are both a - like. The Lamb is the light of the cit - y of God. Shine in my heart, Lord Je - sus.

157   Christ in Me Is to Live

TEXT and MUSIC: Gary Garcia

joy. He's my strength,_____ he's my sword,_____
_____ He's my peace, he's my Lord.

Blessing and Honor 158
(3-part canon)

I
Bless - ing and hon - or and glo - ry be yours;

II
Wor - thy are you, O Lord, to re - ceive end - less praise;

III
Bless - ing and hon - or and glo - ry be yours.

TEXT: Gerald S. Henderson; based on Revelation 5:12, 13
MUSIC: German Folk song; adapted by Gerald S. Henderson
GERMAN FOLK
10.12.10.

159　All Things Are Yours

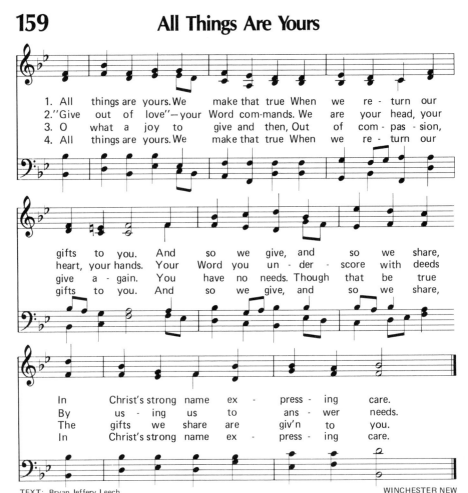

1. All things are yours. We make that true When we re - turn our
2. "Give out of love"— your Word com-mands. We are your head, your
3. O what a joy to give and then, Out of com - pas - sion,
4. All things are yours. We make that true When we re - turn our

gifts to you. And so we give, and so we share,
heart, your hands. Your Word you un - der - score with deeds
give a - gain. You have no needs. Though that be true
gifts to you. And so we give, and so we share,

In Christ's strong name ex - press - ing care.
By us - ing us to ans - wer needs.
The gifts we share are giv'n to you.
In Christ's strong name ex - press - ing care.

TEXT: Bryan Jeffery Leech
MUSIC: Adapted from "Musikalisches Handbuch," Hamburg, 1690
Text copyright © 1989 by Hope Publishing Company, Carol Stream, IL 60188.
All rights reserved. Used by permission.

WINCHESTER NEW
L.M.

160　Glory Be to the Father
(Gloria Patri)

Unison

Glo - ry be to the Fa - ther, glo - ry be to the Son, glo - ry

TEXT: Lesser Doxology (Gloria Patri) c. 4th cent.
MUSIC: John Erickson
Copyright © 1973 by Highland Park Methodist Church, Dallas, Texas 75205.
All rights reserved. Used by permission.

ERICKSON

Whosoe'er Anywhere 161

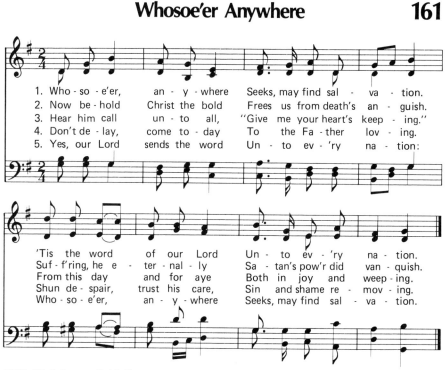

TEXT: Nils Frykman; tr. Karl A. Olsson
MUSIC: Nils Frykman
Words copyright © 1978 by Covenant Publications

OPEN DOOR
6.6.6.6.

162   Give Thanks

Give thanks with a grate-ful heart. Give thanks to the

ho - ly One;__ Give thanks be-cause he's giv - en__ Je - sus

Christ,__ his Son.__ Give Son.__ And

now let the weak say, "I am strong;" let the poor say,

"I am rich" be-cause of what the Lord has done for__

TEXT and MUSIC: Henry Smith, arr. Jonathan D. Larson.
Copyright 1978 Integrity's Hosanna! Music. All rights reserved.
International copyright secured. Used by permission.

us._____ And now let the weak say, "I am

strong;" let the poor say, "I am rich" be-cause of

2nd time to Coda

what the Lord has done for_____ us._____ Give

CODA

us._____ Give thanks._____

O How I Love Jesus 163

O how I love Je - sus, O how I love Je - sus,_____

TEXT: Frederick Whitfield
MUSIC: American melody

O how I love Je - sus, Be - cause he first loved me!

164   Have No Fear, Little Flock

1. Have no fear, lit - tle flock; Have no fear, lit - tle
2. Have good cheer, lit - tle flock; Have good cheer, lit - tle
3. Praise the Lord high a - bove; Praise the Lord high a -
4. Thank-ful hearts raise to God; Thank-ful hearts raise to

flock, For the Fa - ther has cho - sen To
flock, For the Fa - ther will keep you In
bove, For he stoops down to heal you, Up -
God, For he stays close be - side you, In

give you the king - dom; Have no fear, lit - tle flock!
his love for - ev - er; Have good cheer, lit - tle flock!
lift and re - store you; Praise the Lord high a - bove!
all things works with you; Thank-ful hearts raise to God!

TEXT: Luke 12:32, st. 1, Marjorie Jillson, sts. 2-4
MUSIC: Heinz Werner Zimmermann
Copyright 1973 Concordia Publishing House. Reprinted by permission.

LITTLE FLOCK
6.6.7.6.6.

Jesu, Jesu, Fill Us with Your Love 165

Je - su, Je - su, fill us with your love, show
us how to serve the neigh-bors we have from you.

Fine

1. Kneels at the feet of his friends, Si - lent - ly wash - es their
2. Neigh-bors are rich and poor, Neigh-bors of ev - 'ry
3. These are the ones we should serve, These are the ones we should
4. Kneel at the feet of our friends, Si - lent - ly wash - ing their

D.C. al Fine

feet, Mas - ter who pours our him - self for them.
race, Neigh-bors are near and far a - way.
love. All are neigh - bors to us and you.
feet, This is the way we should live with you.

TEXT: Tom Colvin
MUSIC: Ghana Folk Song, adapted by Tom Colvin, arr. by Jane Marshall

CHEREPONI
Irregular

166 Worthy Is the Lamb

1. Wor - thy, wor - thy, wor - thy is the Lamb of God.
2. Glo - ry, glo - ry, glo - ry to his ho - ly name.
3. Ho - ly, ho - ly, ho - ly is the Lord our God.
4. Wor - thy, wor - thy, wor - thy is the Lamb of God.

Wor - thy, wor - thy, wor - thy is the Lamb.
Glo - ry, glo - ry, glo - ry to his name.
Ho - ly, ho - ly, ho - ly is the Lord.
Wor - thy, wor - thy, wor - thy is the Lamb.

TEXT and MUSIC: Rick Ridings, based on Revelation 5:12
Copyright © 1975 Rick Ridings. Used by permission.

GOING FORTH

All Through the Day

167

All through the day, all through the night, Dwell in his prom- is-es, walk in his light. Dark - ness shall flee at his com - mand. All through the day and night we're in his hand.

TEXT and MUSIC: Tom Howard

168   In My Life, Lord, Be Glorified

1. In my life, Lord, Be glo-ri-fied, Be glo-ri-fied.
2. In my song, Lord, Be glo-ri-fied, Be glo-ri-fied.
3. In your church, Lord, Be glo-ri-fied, Be glo-ri-fied.

In my life, Lord, Be glo-ri-fied to-day.
In my song, Lord, Be glo-ri-fied to-day.
In your church, Lord, Be glo-ri-fied to-day.

TEXT and MUSIC: Bob Kilpatrick

Sing so as to make the world hear. The highest value of our sing-
ing after all has not been the mere gladness we have felt
because of our salvation, but the joy of pouring out the praises of
our God to those who have not known him, or of arousing them
by our singing to new thoughts and a new life.

And sing till your whole soul is lifted up to God, and then
sing till you lift the eyes of those who know not God to him who
is the foundation of all our joy!

General William Booth

1. Christ is the King! O friends, re - joice, Broth-ers and
2. O mag - ni - fy the Lord, and raise An - thems of
3. They with a faith for - ev - er new Fol - lowed the
4. O Chris - tian wom - en, Chris - tian men, All the world
5. Christ through all a - ges is the same: Place the same
6. Let love's un - con - quer - a - ble might Your scat-tered

sis - ters with one voice Let the world know he is your choice.
joy and ho - ly praise For Christ's brave saints of an-cient days.
King, and round him drew Thou-sands of ser - vants brave and true.
o - ver, seek a - gain The way dis - ci - ples fol - lowed then.
hope in his great name, With the same faith his Word pro - claim;
com - pan - ies u - nite In ser - vice to the Lord of light;

Al - le - lu - ia! Al - le - lu - ia! Al - le - lu - ia!
Al - le - lu - ia! Al - le - lu - ia! Al - le - lu - ia!
Al - le - lu - ia! Al - le - lu - ia! Al - le - lu - ia!
Al - le - lu - ia! Al - le - lu - ia! Al - le - lu - ia!
Al - le - lu - ia! Al - le - lu - ia! Al - le - lu - ia!
Al - le - lu - ia! Al - le - lu - ia! Al - le - lu - ia!

TEXT: G. K. A. Bell
MUSIC: M. Vulpius

GELOBT SEI GOTT
8.8.8. with alleluias

170   # On Our Way Rejoicing

1. On our way re - joic - ing Glad - ly let us go.
2. Un - to God the Fa - ther Joy - ful songs we sing;

Christ our Lord has con - quered; Van-quished is the foe.
Un - to God the Sav - ior Thank-ful hearts we bring;

Christ with-out, our safe - ty; Christ with-in, our joy;
Un - to God the Spir - it Bow we and a - dore,

TEXT: John S. B. Monsell
MUSIC: Frances R. Havergal
Arr. copyright 1978 Lutheran Book of Worship.
Reprinted by permission of Augsburg Fortress.

HERMAS
6.5.6.5.D with refrain

Who, if we be faith - ful, Can our hope de - stroy?
On our way re - joic - ing Now and ev - er - more.

REFRAIN

On our way re - joic - ing; As we for - ward move,

Hear - ken to our prais - es, O blest God of love!

171   O Let the Son of God Enfold You
(Spirit Song)

1. O let the Son of God en-fold you with his Spir-it and his love, let him fill your life and sat-is-fy your soul. O let him have the things that hold you and his Spir-it like a

2. O come and sing the song with glad-ness as your hearts are filled with joy, lift your hands in sweet sur-ren-der to his name. O give him all your tears and sad-ness, give him all your years of

TEXT and MUSIC: John Wimber

172 Freely, Freely

1. God for - gave my sin in Je - sus'
(2.) pow'r is giv'n in Je - sus'

name, I've been born a - gain in Je - sus'
name, in earth and heav'n in Je - sus'

name. And in Je - sus' name I come to
name. And in Je - sus' name I come to

you to share his love as he told me
you to share his pow'r as he told me

173

You Shall Go Out with Joy
(The Trees of the Field)

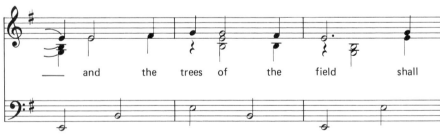

TEXT: Steffi Geiser Rubin, based on Isaiah 55:12
MUSIC: Stuart Dauerman

174 Let the Words of the Lord

(Colossians 3:17)

TEXT and MUSIC: James Black, arr. Richard K. Carlson

all
all in the name____ of the Lord Je - sus Christ who
Walk

rose from the dead to give you new life in him.

Shalom

175

(2-part canon)

Sha - lom, good friends, sha - lom, good friends, Sha - lom, sha - lom. Till

we meet a-gain, till we meet a - gain, Sha - lom, sha - lom.

TEXT: Ancient Hebrew benediction
MUSIC: Hebrew melody

176   Through the Heart of Ev'ry City

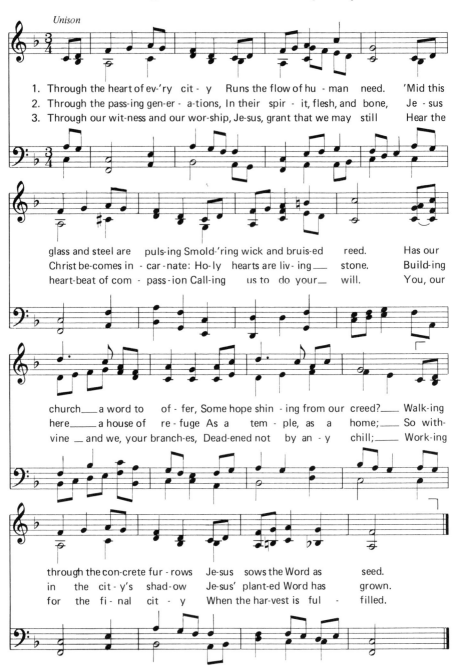

Unison

1. Through the heart of ev-'ry cit - y Runs the flow of hu - man need. 'Mid this
2. Through the pass-ing gen-er - a-tions, In their spir - it, flesh, and bone, Je - sus
3. Through our wit-ness and our wor-ship, Je-sus, grant that we may still Hear the

glass and steel are puls-ing Smold-'ring wick and bruis-ed reed. Has our
Christ be-comes in - car-nate: Ho-ly hearts are liv - ing___ stone. Build-ing
heart-beat of com - pass-ion Call-ing us to do your___ will. You, our

church___ a word to of - fer, Some hope shin - ing from our creed?___ Walk-ing
here___ a house of re - fuge As a tem - ple, as a home;___ So with-
vine ___ and we, your branch-es, Dead-ened not by an - y chill;___ Work-ing

through the con-crete fur - rows Je-sus sows the Word as seed.
in the cit - y's shad-ow Je-sus' plant-ed Word has grown.
for the fi - nal cit - y When the har-vest is ful - filled.

TEXT: Sylvia Dunstan
MUSIC: William P. Rowan
Text copyright by William P. Rowan. Harm. copyright © 1989 by A. Royce Eckhardt.
Used by permission.

TRUESDELL
8.7.8.7.D.

Go Now in Peace

TEXT and MUSIC: Natalie Sleeth, 1975
Copyright © 1976 by Hinshaw Music, Inc. Reprinted by permission 6-7-89.

GO NOW IN PEACE

INDEXES

TOPICAL BY CATEGORIES

44:3	63	9:27-30	59	3:5-8	63
48:17,18	140	10:8	172	:14-15	97
49:10	120	11:28	148,152	4:10	127
:15	86	12:40	95	:13-14	171
:26	83	13:3-9	176	:24	1
51:10	42	15:30-31	76	:25-26	83
52:7	108	18:20	114	:46-53	76
:10	15	19:13-15	148	6:32-35	120
53:2,3	108	20:29-34	17,59	:29-58	38
55:6,7	152	22:41-45	17,39	:48-58	113,120
:12	117,173	26:26-28	120	7:16-17	82
57:15-19	164	:61	95	:37	113
61:3	117	27:38-40	95	8:12	111
:6	98	28:1-10	95	:28	97
65:13	47	:10	96	:32	66
66:13	86	:18-20	172	:32,36	46
		:20	38	:58	32
Jeremiah				9	59
10:12	43	Mark		10:3	123
11:5	74	1:3	15	:11-16	68
31:10	68	:12-13	77	11:22	5,114
:13	145	4:28-29	95	12:28	20
		4:39	109	:32	84
Lamentations		8:31	95	:32,34	97
3:22,23	101	10:18	64	13:3-5	165
:23	75	14:22-24	120	14:1-3	135
		:58	95	:1-4	148
Ezekiel		16	95	:1-6	82
20:6,15	74			:6	139
36:26	151	Luke		:16,25,26	83
		1:26-38	90	:17	63
Hosea		:46-55	147	:25-28	109
6:1,2	76	:68-75	27	15:1-5	176
		2:1-7	90	:1-8	80
Joel		:1-20	91,92,94	:1-11	146
2:21-27	54	:39-40	90	:9,13	130
:28,29	63	3:1-12	129	20:1-18	95
		:4	15	:19-20,24-28	108
Habbakuk		4:1-13	77	:27	82
2:14	4	:40	76		
3:18	47,170	:40-44	17	Acts	
		9:57-62	8	1:3-9	38
Malachi		10:25-37	165	:11	87
3:1	15	11:13	63	2:1-21	63
4:2	102,156	12:27	115,117	:21	161
		:32	164	:24	85
Matthew		13:29	128	4:12	31
1:23	17,23,72	19:41	176	8:39	170
2:1-11	94	20:41-44	17	9:8	59
:2	155	22:14-22	119,128	17:24	43
:14	93	:17-20	125	26:18	59,161
3	129	:19-20	120		
:3	15	23:42	122	Romans	
4:1-11	77	24:1-10	95	3:3-4	100
:23	76	:13-35	121	:24	46
:23-25	17	:30-32	128	5:17	46
5:12	170	:31	59	6:5-14	149
:13-16	1	:34	40,96	8:1-27	63
:16	168			8:31-39	42,85,150
6:9-13	67	John		10:11-13	161
:28	102,115,117	1:1-5	23	12:4	43
:33	5,114	:4	111	15:5-6	32
8:12	128	:4-5,9	127	:7-9	97
:16-17	76	2:19-20	95	:33	177

MEDLEY INDEX

Praise and worship will flow more smoothly if songs are sung in sequence, without interruption. These medleys will usually be related in key, tempo, and theme. You may wish to create your own medleys on occasion. A possible sequence might be: opening, celebration, praise, worship, adoration, and prayer. It is good to begin with songs that talk *about* God, and move into songs that talk *to* God.

Here is a list of suggested medleys with their keys:

GATHERING

5	Seek Ye First	D
6	Be Still and Know	D
9	Bless the Lord	G,A^b
10	Lift Up Your Heads	A^b
11	He Is Lord	A^b

PRAISE

20	Father, We Love You	C
21	Bless the Lord	F
22	For Thou, O Lord	F
23	Jesus, Name above	F
24	Great Is the Lord	C
25	How Majestic	C
27	I Will Call	D
28	I Will Sing	D
29	There Is Strength	G,A^b

30	Behold, What Manner	D
31	Praise the Name	D
32	We Will Glorify	D,E^b
33	Majesty	B^b
34	To God Be the Glory	B^b
47	Rejoice in the Lord	F
48	Alleluia, Alleluia	F

PRAYER

58	Lord, Listen	D
59	Open Our Eyes	D
60	I Love You, Lord	D,G
61	Adoramus Te	G

SACRAMENTS

130	O How He Loves	A
122	Jesus, Remember Me	D

WITNESS

134	Love Divine, So Great	G
135	Sing the Wondrous Love	C

Familiar hymns or refrains could also be added to medleys. Here are some which might be sung from memory. Instrumentalists would probably need the written music. The usual key is included:

G	Amazing Grace
G	Doxology (several versions)
B^b	For Thine Is the Kingdom (Lord's Prayer ending, Malotte)
D	Great Is Thy Faithfulness
D	Joy to the World
A^b	O Come, Let Us Adore Him (O Come All Ye Faithful)
A^b	O For a Thousand Tongues to Sing
A^b	Praise the Lord (To God Be the Glory)
D	This is My Story (Blessed Assurance)
B^b	Then Sings My Soul (How Great Thou Art)

ALPHABETICAL/FIRST LINES AND TITLES
(Titles in italics)